Praise for *It Doesn't End Here*

"A heart wrenching story of a mother's transcendent love for her young son, and the faith which enabled her to survive his tragic death. There is a lot to be learned from this moving narrative: about spiritual warfare, about the callousness of the pharmaceutical industry and its legal apparatus, about the role of faith and prayer in sustaining our lives, and most of all about how the Blessed Virgin Mary, in the suffering she endured at the foot of the Cross, makes it possible for us, too, to bear our crosses."

—Roy Schoeman, bestselling author of *Salvation Is From The Jews* and *Honey From The Rock*

"I know on a personal level the depth of Dawn Marie's loss, having unexpectedly lost my own precious 21-year old son a year ago. Her unwavering faith and strength through her long ordeal has been a real inspiration to me. My heart goes out to her as a mom who understands what she has both lost and gained by the stand she's taken so others can be spared the heartbreak she and her family have suffered.

It Doesn't End Here is a 'must read' for anyone who is struggling with loss, especially that of a child. Dawn Marie's honesty and courage will move, inspire and uplift you, as it did me."

—April Rovero, Founder/President, *National Coalition Against Prescription Drug Abuse* www.ncapda.org

"Sooner or later we all arrive at a moment in our lives that seems all too big for us. How will you deal with yours? *It Doesn't End Here* will prepare you for that moment when it comes. This is a message of incredible light in the midst of all consuming darkness."

—Matthew Kelly, New York Times bestselling author of *The Rhythm of Life* and *The Dream Manager*

"A testimony of how faith can survive the most extreme and tragic circumstances."

—Michael H. Brown, bestselling
The God of M

"This book is an amazing tale of faith, persistence, and love. The unimaginable events that led to her son Nathaniel's death could have broken her. Instead, Dawn Marie Roeder embarked on a journey to help others avoid tragedy by warning them of the unusual side effects of her ADHD medication. She persisted for years, showing incredible strength in fighting the big-moneyed pharmaceutical company. When tragedy strikes an individual's life, and there is none worse than the loss of a child, there is a choice to be made—to go on or to succumb to depression. Dawn Marie's story is a testimony to resilience."

—Ellen M. Diana, Ph.D. Psychologist and Author of *Charge Up Your Life: Conquer the 6 Barriers to Love, Happiness and Success*

"From the perspective of a spiritual father, Dawn Marie's story brings me great joy. She has found the path to holiness: the way of the Cross. The Lord has opened her eyes to the mystery of his great love.

As you journey through her story, keep an open mind and an open heart. Invite the Lord into your life and ask him to show you your life through the lens of the Paschal Mystery. I promise, you will not be disappointed. What you will discover is the incredible truth that has led Dawn Marie to title her book, *It Doesn't End Here*!"

—Reverend William D. Schmid, M.A.

"Dawn Marie Roeder's personal story takes us on an reflective journey of the painful and tragic loss of her son in a car accident after she suffered an adverse reaction to a prescription drug; then through the ensuing and brutal assassination of her character in court by the legal counsel of the pharmaceutical company she held accountable.

Roeder's survival of these events—let alone her miraculous recovery and attitude—is a testimony of her devotion to her Catholic faith and the God she serves. Her victory resonates with the Holy Spirit and gives us comfort and hope that our own seemingly senseless tragedies can also be transformed with God's love and forgiveness."

—Gwen Olsen, Author of *Confessions of an Rx Drug Pusher: God's Call to Loving Arms*

"Struggling to find meaning out of the unimaginable circumstances that lead to her son's tragic death, Dawn Marie strove daily to put back together the shattered remains of her life one second at a time. Six months into the journey of her great torment Dawn's mother hands her a newspaper article which lead to a discovery that would dramatically alter her life and the lives of many others.

In this true story of pain and sorrow is found an amazing love of a mother for her son and an enduring faith in an ever present loving God."

—FR. DONALD CALLOWAY, AUTHOR OF
NO TURNING BACK: A WITNESS TO MERCY

"Dawn Marie demonstrated tremendous strength of character to write her memoir, *It Doesn't End Here.* It relives a heartbreaking event with such honesty and clarity about the lessons she learned. Dawn Marie's words uplift and inspire others to overcome grief and to forgive—just as she did."

—ANDREA MARKOWITZ, PH.D, EDITOR, AT *WRITE FOR YOUR BUSINESS*

"Author Dawn Marie Roeder addresses a tough subject in her new book, *It Doesn't End Here.* This is a beautiful book for anyone who has lost a child, either through abortion, natural causes or unfortunate circumstances.

Dawn addresses subjects such as faith, forgiveness and hope. Dawn lost her little boy Nathaniel in a series of events that would change her life forever. She draws upon trauma in her life including a past abortion to paint a beautiful picture of how one can overcome deep tragedy with faith and hope in the Lord. Dawn adds a very personal touch to the book including journal entries that really pull the reader in.

We recommend this book to anyone who has gone through trauma in their life, especially trauma involving the loss of a child. *It Doesn't End Here* will deepen your faith and give you hope."

—*RACHEL'S VINEYARD: VINE AND BRANCHES NEWSLETTER, MARCH 2010 ISSUE*

It Doesn't End Here

An Amazing Journey of Faith and Forgiveness

Dawn Marie Roeder

7/1/16
To: Henry:
Siempre adelante!
Keep moving forward!
Blessings in Christ +
Love of Mary!
Dawn Marie

It Doesn't End Here: An Amazing Journey of Faith and Forgiveness
by Dawn Marie Roeder
www.ItDoesntEndHere.com

For information about this title contact the publisher:
Lanciano Media LLC
office@LancianoMedia.com

Library of Congress Control Number: 2009910567
ISBN: 978-0-9842444-1-6
Printed in the United States of America

Cover Design: Claudia Volkman
Interior Illustration: Steve and Linda Voita
Interior Photograph courtesy of the author
Interior Design: 1106 Design

Dedicated

to

Our Lady and Her Son Our Lord Jesus,

my son Nathaniel who continues to inspire me

and

to all the suffering sojourners of life,

"Do Not Fear To Hope!"

Disclaimer

Dawn Marie Roeder is an average person who has experienced a life-altering event. This is her personal account of past events and her memories, along with those of family and friends. Dawn Marie holds a firm belief that when taken by patients and administered and monitored properly by professionals, medication can aid immensely in raising the quality of one's life. Dawn is not an authority on any medical conditions, nor is she a trained medical professional. The information in this book is not offered to influence anyone to ignore professional medical advice, or go against a medical program established by professionals for individual patients. Individuals should check with their personal physicians or caretakers before changing any medical program established by professionals.

CONTENTS

FOREWORD

As a Catholic priest, one of the more difficult challenges of my ministry is helping the people of God unite their sufferings with the sufferings of the crucified Christ. More often than not human suffering is interpreted as either proof of the non-existence of God or as God's abandonment of humanity. A common question that priests hear on a regular basis is, "If God loves me, why is there so much pain and suffering in my life?" The presumption behind this question is that pain and suffering do not belong to the mystery of love; love is safe and leads people away from harm. Yet, anyone who has ever loved another person knows that this is not the case. Love is dangerous, risky business. Love demands both sacrifice and vulnerability, two things that are often accompanied by pain and suffering. True love beckons us to open ourselves up and give ourselves away, even to the point of physical pain.

Is this not the kind of love proclaimed in the Gospel of John? "For God so loved the world that he gave his only Son so that those who believe in him might not perish but have eternal life" (John 3:16). God loves humanity so much that he opens himself up (becomes vulnerable) and gives his life (sacrifices himself) so that we might have the fullness of life. God's love for humanity is so powerful that he suffers physical pain and death so that we can receive the fullness of his blessings. The Cross of Christ is the ultimate sign of love. It is the greatest act of love the world has ever seen. Yet, at the same time, it is an act in no way deprived of immense pain and suffering.

The most profound truth that I have come to experience in my life is that it is precisely the suffering of Christ on the Cross that makes Christianity so special and unique. The Cross of Christ gives meaning and purpose to suffering: those who suffer and die with Christ will also rise with him. On account of the crucified Christ, human suffering is no longer merely one of the consequences of a cruel world that must be overcome, but an opportunity for spiritual growth. Every cross endured in this life is a chance to grow closer to God. Every suffering that we bear patiently is an opportunity to grow in holiness. In this way, suffering is redemptive. Each and every suffering is an opportunity to unite ourselves to the sufferings of Christ so as to experience the power of his resurrection and the new life that comes with it. In this way, human suffering is not a sign of God's disinterest in us or his abandonment of humanity. Rather, God is so invested in his people that he takes the most painful human experiences and transforms them so that they can give profound meaning to our lives. Those who experience great sufferings are capable of great faith.

It is this notion of redemptive suffering that makes Dawn Marie's story worth telling. As you will discover, Dawn Marie's story is filled with pain and suffering. She suffered the pains of losing the one person she loved the most: her son, Nathaniel. Yet, through her great loss, Dawn Marie has come to a profound understanding of the love of God. In a mysterious way, the tragedy she experienced has given her life a new meaning and purpose. Her story takes us on a journey from death to new life, and at every stage of this journey Dawn Marie shows us how she united her sufferings to the sufferings of the crucified Christ through the intercession of the Blessed Mother. The seven sorrows of Mary are the means by which she accomplishes this great feat.

From the perspective of a spiritual father, Dawn Marie's story brings me great joy. She has found the path to holiness: the way of the Cross. The Lord has opened her eyes to the mystery of his great love. My hope for all who read her story is that they will learn from her. All of us are called to unite ourselves to the sufferings of Christ. It is the mission and goal of every Christian. Dawn Marie's story has much to teach us about this. As you journey through Dawn Marie's story, keep an open mind and an open heart. Invite the Lord into your life and ask him to show you your life through the lens of the Paschal Mystery. I promise, you will not be disappointed. What you will discover is the incredible truth that has led Dawn Marie to title her book, *It Doesn't End Here!*

Reverend William D. Schmid, M.A.
October 1, 2009
Feast of St. Therese of Lisieux

INTRODUCTION

POPE JOHN PAUL II DECLARED the year 2000 a Year of Jubilee for the Catholic Church. At the age of thirty four, this year did not bring for me the joyous celebration that I, who was born and baptized as a Catholic, had hoped for. Instead, it reigned in the complete opposite. On March 18, during the Catholic season of Lent, I would experience my very own "way of the cross" when my only son, Nathaniel Joseph, died by way of a most tragic set of circumstances.

The story I tell is not one I had ever wanted to write. Putting pen to paper ushered in for me a tsunami of tears that at times caught me off guard. I write in the hopes that out of my experience the reader may gain a greater appreciation for the precious gifts each has in his or her own life. It is a story about good verses evil. A person may not believe in the existence of evil or hell. I do. I can attest to hell because I've been there. Not in the "other" worldly sense, but in the harrowing experience of tragic loss, and in encountering individuals who had masqueraded on the side of good but who profoundly lacked an honest connection with empathy and shame.

Yet I write as one who has great hope, because as much as I have been witness to serious evil, I have been blessed to experience the miraculous in both the ordinary and extraordinary circumstances of everyday life. These are the experiences I am eager to share. Out of care and concern I have taken the precaution of changing the names to protect the people involved. Also I refer to the prescription medication as: prescription medication or prescription drug and the pharmaceutical company as pharmaceutical company or corporation.

As a young child growing up in Wilkes-Barre, Pennsylvania, I can remember perching myself on my bedroom windowsill, gazing at the stars, and being swept up by the luminous way the moon shone in the black sky. I often felt the need to share my joy of the night sky, and so I sang my little heart out in made-up songs to Jesus and Mary. The bedside prayers my parents taught me stirred in me the passion to pray every night for all my relatives and friends who needed prayers.

My curiosity about discovering God was always there. One Sunday at church, after joyfully scanning every nook and cranny of my surroundings, I tugged on my mom's skirt. With eagerness and a sense of urgency I asked her, "Where's undergod?" After a few more tugs on her skirt, she leaned down and asked me what I meant. Puzzled by her question, I said, "You know!" and placing my hand on my heart I started to say the Pledge of Allegiance, "'...and to the Republic for which it stands, one nation *undergod*, indivisible'—Where's *undergod*?" Thanks to *Romper Room*, the children's television show where I learned the Pledge of Allegiance, she got a good laugh from my misunderstanding of the words.

The joy I remember in singing those songs and praying for my family, and from my curious spirit remain with me until this day as I reflect back on what I believe is the Holy Spirit's guidance, protection and affection being expressed and felt in my heart.

I derived inspiration and encouragement while writing my story, *It Doesn't End Here,* from the twelfth-century Servite Devotion of the Seven Sorrows of Mary. Many years before I even dared to write this book, and as I journeyed through my pain trying to rebuild my challenged faith life, I attended events that provided opportunities for spiritual growth and inspiration to aid in the process of mending my wounded heart and mind. At one such event there was a priest who was speaking about Mary the Mother of Jesus and her role in our lives today. There were about five hundred people gathered at the event.

The priest gave a wonderful talk and afterward he invited those gathered in attendance to ask any questions they might have. Many people began to raise their hands and asked him questions. As I sat in the back corner of the room I too desired to ask him something, but I believed there would be only a slight chance I would get to ask it because I was sitting so far in the back of the room. Also, I was unsure what it was exactly I wanted to ask him and I was fearful of what his response might be.

I had a choice to make, and so I took a deep breath and gathered what courage I had within me. Reaching out, perhaps feeling what the woman who grabbed onto the tassel of the Lord had felt in a large crowd, I raised my hand. To my astonishment, he called on me. What came out of my mouth felt more like a ramble. But I did it; I opened my mouth and spoke the following:

> *Father, if it is that Our God has sent as an example here among us, the Mother of God to shake us from complacency and guide us on the way to Her Son how then can you explain how it can ever be that I expect to take the tragic situation in which I find myself, which is the death of my only son, and see any possible good in it?*

He looked toward me and responded:

> *Because Our Lady walked this path before you, know it is possible. Though your child was taken from you, it does not mean you are meant to be any less happy in life than anyone else—just that your walk is more amazing. You obviously need to walk the side of the mountain Our Lady walked more dramatically than others.*

The moment the priest's last word was spoken hundreds of people in the room turned to look at me, perhaps awaiting my reaction to his response. I sat struck in wonder at his statement and most particularly at the word "amazing." I said to myself, *did he just say amazing? AMAZING? How could this situation possibly EVER be amazing?* Still, I derived peace and strength from his words, thinking, *She walked there before me. Know it is possible.*

Nathaniel was born on November 10, 1997 at Scottsdale Memorial Hospital Osborn. His coming was without any major complications. My water broke at midnight. About midway through my attempt to be "strong" and have a natural childbirth, all it took was the nurse on duty to whisper in my ear something about my not having to try and be a hero, and I screamed "EPIDURAL!" Several hours later at noon, the joy of my life was born.

I remember how incredible it was that Nathaniel never left my sight after he was born. The nurses took him from the doctor, bathed him in the very room in which he was born and then placed him in my arms. My heart nearly leaped out of my chest when I gazed into his beautiful face for the first time. His cheeks were rosy and full, his lips puckered red as garnet, and when his eyes met mine at last, I was speechless.

What blessed emotions I felt when his tiny little fingers clutched mine. As his little mouth searched for sustenance from my breast, I was humbled at the sacredness of this moment which nurtured him. As he sighed in my arms, I also sighed and felt for a moment that our hearts beat in unison, the same rhythm of peace and contentment.

I prayed often, thanking God for this precious gift named Nathaniel Joseph. I knew he was to be named Nathaniel the moment I heard this name mentioned during a dinner conversation. I cannot tell you exactly why, but when I heard the name Nathaniel spoken, it was as if I had heard it for the first time and I knew this was to be his name. Nathaniel means "gift from God" and Joseph "to be added." How appropriate, as this gift from God was graciously added to our family.

The reader may find it helpful to approach reading my story in two ways. If familiar with the Sorrows of Mary, he or she may want to skip the introduction to each chapter, which begins with a meditation on the particular sorrow, and jump right into the story. Or the reader may wish to read both, as in the Sorrows, I hope, he or she will find, as I myself found, strength from Mary's journey. I end each chapter with a fond memory of my son.

Although I'm inspired by Mary, I don't pretend to compare myself to the Mother of God. As the reader will soon see, a pedestal is not where I belong. I share my story from the need of my own personal faith and experience and for the love of my son Nathaniel. My thanks for taking time to read my side of the story.

Consecration

THIS BOOK WAS CONSECRATED TO GOD on the Feast day of Our Lady of Sorrows, September 15, during Mass at Our Lady of Perpetual Help Church in Scottsdale, Arizona.

Our Lady Of Sorrows—Feast (September 15)

This feast dates back to the twelfth century. It was especially promoted by the Cistercians and the Servites, so much so that in the fourteenth and fifteenth centuries it was widely celebrated throughout the Catholic church. In 1482 the feast was added to the Missal under the title of *"Our Lady of Compassion."* Pope Benedict XIII added it to the Roman Calendar in 1727 on the Friday before Palm Sunday. In 1913 Pope Pius X fixed the date on September 15. The title *"Our Lady of Sorrows"* focuses on Mary's intense suffering during the passion and death of Christ. "The Seven Dolors," the title by which it was celebrated in the seventeenth century, referred to the seven swords that pierced the Heart of Mary.

The author wishes to affirm her unconditional submission to the final and official judgment of the magisterium of the church regarding the events presently under investigation at Medjugorje.

SEVEN SORROWS

I. Simeon's Prophecy at the Presentation of Jesus (St. Luke 2:34, 35)
II. The Flight with Jesus into Egypt (St. Matthew 2:13–14)
III. The Loss of her Son, Jesus, in Jerusalem (St. Luke 2:43–45)
IV. The Meeting with her Son, Jesus, on the Way to Calvary
V. The Agony and Death of her Son, Jesus, on the Cross
VI. Jesus is Taken Down from the Cross and placed in her arms
VII. The Burial of her Son, Jesus

1 Thessalonians 4:13–18

We do not want you to be unaware, brothers, about those who have fallen asleep, so that you may not grieve like the rest, who have no hope.

For if we believe that Jesus died and rose, so too will God, through Jesus, bring with him those who have fallen asleep.

Indeed, we tell you this, on the word of the Lord, that we who are alive, who are left until the coming of the Lord, will surely not precede those who have fallen asleep.

For the Lord himself, with a word of command, with the voice of an archangel and with the trumpet of God, will come down from heaven, and the dead in Christ will rise first.

Then we who are alive, who are left, will be caught up together with them in the clouds to meet the Lord in the air. Thus we shall always be with the Lord.

Therefore, console one another with these words.

First Sorrow
Luke 2:35

"And you yourself a sword will pierce"

I wonder how frightened Mary became after hearing the words of the Prophet Simeon, forecasting the fate of her child, along with her own, their lives inextricably woven together. He will be "a light for revelation to the Gentiles, and glory for your people Israel."[1]

How amazed Mary must have been at first to hear this prediction...but then Simeon continued: "this child is destined for the fall and rise of many in Israel and to be a sign that will be contradicted."[2]

Perhaps she thought something like this: *That doesn't sound very positive. What does this mean? He might not be liked or even loved by all. I know the Old Testament very well. My parents made certain I went to temple every day to study. Joyfully I went. I remember the words of the Prophet Isaiah:* "a grave was assigned Him among the wicked, a burial place with evildoers, though he had done no wrong, nor spoken any falsehood."[3]

Simeon continued with his prophecy: "and you yourself a sword will pierce, so that the thoughts of many hearts may be revealed."[4]

How puzzled Mary might have felt: *The presentation of my son is to be a joyous time. According to our custom he is consecrated to God. What does this mean that a sword will pierce my heart? Why am I presented with a sword and not a rose or a lily in celebration? I can handle a thorn from a rose but not a sword. What suffering is in store for my precious child? What awaits Him? Mind not my suffering but his. I cannot bear to think of it, but TRUST. I trust you my heavenly Father...I do not understand you but I trust in your will.*

"...and his mother kept all these things in her heart."[5]

One

Driven To Destruction

"Will somebody tell me where I am, please?!! What the hell is going on? Why am I strapped to this (explicative) table? Please, please, somebody tell me what is going on! Water, water, I need water!"

A nurse was standing by in the room.

"Please give me a drink of water. I'm going to die of thirst here. Would you please give me a [I cursed again] drink of water?" I think I'm in a hospital. Why the hell won't this damn nurse give me a drink of water?

Writhing and screaming accusations at the nurse, I tried to break loose from the straps. The horrible sense of dehydration was magnified by the psychotic break that was running its course. I tried to bargain with the nurse.

"Okay then, just a sip, *please*. If you won't give me a glass of water then just a drop on my tongue...I don't need a full glass."

I pleaded in pathetic desperation.

"Would somebody in this damn place please give me a drop of water?!"

It was 10:30 am, Saturday morning, on March 18 of 2000 that my life had been changed forever. My son Nathaniel and I had been in a terrible car accident. The nurse had not yet drawn blood as I had only arrived at John C. Lincoln Hospital by helicopter. My son Nathaniel had been flown to St. Joseph's Hospital because they specialized in treating young children. There was something drastically wrong with my behavior and as a standard procedure, blood needed to be drawn. I had no memory of being flown to the hospital or of the reason why such transport was necessary.

According to family and friends I had been acting strangely that entire week, with my behavior escalating into hostility and aggression and my speech accusatory and suspicious. My parents told me I had been verbally attacking my dad's brother, my favorite uncle, John, who was visiting us from Pennsylvania. I started calling him the devil. My friends Cindy and Michael said that I was "over-spiritualizing" everything. Since I had always been very passionate about my faith life and had served in several ministries, my "overly–spiritual" behavior did not fully catch my parents' and friends' attention. However, they later said that in the back of their minds they knew something was wrong, but could not put their fingers on it.

The local news stations reported the horrific events: *Badly injured child flown to St. Joseph's Hospital while unknown woman flown to John C. Lincoln Hospital.* The firemen and police at the scene of the accident had a difficult time retrieving sensible information from me. Earlier that morning I had rushed out of the house in bare feet with Nathaniel cradled under my arm for what I believed was his rescue from the "devil." Thanks be to God there were no major injuries in the car with which we had collided.

"I can't breathe." I was gurgling on blood from the shattered windshield glass which had torn a gaping hole in my jaw. "Help me, I can't breathe!" Somebody had placed a plastic breathing apparatus down my throat. My thinking was still distorted at this point. I believed that the nurse was a devil, trying to kill me. I continued to writhe and scream horrible things at him. He asked to be transferred to another patient since my attacks on him did not stop. After the standard procedures were completed in the emergency room I was taken to the Intensive Care Unit.

My family, having finally been contacted by the police, arrived at John C. Lincoln's Intensive Care Unit at 1:00 pm. As I fought for what was left of my sanity, I was completely unaware of Nathaniel's state and did not ask about him. My parents were confused by this. For several days I remained incoherent and unresponsive to what had happened to me or my son. I kept telling my mom over and over again, "I can't see the forest for the trees, I can't see the forest for the trees." I was in a state of utter chaos and confusion.

Dr. Phillips, the reconstructive surgeon, after making his observation, noted in his records on the day of my arrival, "...tested positive for amphetamines, evaluated by neurology for significant confusion, ranting about Jesus and Satan." Because of my uncooperative behavior, Dr. Phillips made the decision to wait until the next morning to operate on my broken nose and close the wound in my jaw.

"Dawn." My mother tried to get information from me after the doctors reported finding narcotics in my blood stream.

"Yes Mom?"

"Were you taking medication?"

"Yes Mom."

"What were you taking?"

"I was taking my thyroid medication and my prescription medication."

"What is your prescription medication?" My mom had to ask me.

"It's for my attention deficit disorder."

At the time of the accident I was a single mom and I wanted to provide the best life for my son. I had decided to go back to graduate school. Because I had struggled with distraction in high school and in my undergraduate studies I had decided to seek help. After extensive testing and examination from an internationally known attention deficit disorder specialist a few years earlier, I thought I should keep an open mind and try a medication. I was embarrassed about needing medication; therefore I never told my family that I was taking it. Their first time hearing about it was in the hospital after the accident.

My History With Attention Deficit Disorder

In 1998 I received a diagnosis of attention deficit disorder from a well-known clinic that specialized in treating individuals with attention deficit disorder and attention deficit hyperactivity disorder. I had been through extensive testing which included written tests, visual continuous-performance computer-generated tests and neurological tests that mapped brain activity while I performed simple to complex exercises such as eyes open, eyes shut, reading and math. According to the clinic director, the topographs that charted my brain-wave activity, known as EEDs, so typified an individual with attention deficit disorder that he asked if he could use copies of my topographs on his advertisement brochures. The brochures were to be placed at libraries and meeting halls where he lectured. I gave him my permission.

It was important for me to be thorough and seek a proper diagnosis. I was an average student in junior high and high school. It was challenging for me to see my friends excel while I just got by with nominal grades. I tended to be a daydreamer. I knew I had it in me to do better than I was doing, but I didn't quite know how to do it. It wasn't until my undergraduate work in college that I developed techniques of my own, to filter out distractions and limit the procrastination that typifies individuals with ADD. My motivation to improve my academic standing came when a professor at college orientation said we could expect to see our grade point averages remain the same as they were throughout our junior high and high school years. That comment inspired me and I took it as a challenge to prove the theory wrong.

One of the techniques I used to heighten my ability to focus was to move to the front seat of every class. This was a huge benefit for me. My grades began to improve. I enjoyed class and participated more. Another technique I used was tape recording classes that I found less stimulating. When I did this, instead of putting stress on myself to pay attention to every detail, I knew I had the recording to fall back on, which enabled me to listen more while taking notes at a comfortable pace. Another thing I did to limit distractions was to place earplugs in my ears while taking tests. Before using these methods, I would get frustrated with classroom noises. How wonderful it was to now be more focused and drown out the sounds of papers shuffling and tapping pencils, sneezing, coughing and whispers.

As my grade point average climbed from a 2.7 to 3.5 and eventually to 4.0 four semesters in a row, I noticed another benefit: my self-esteem rose with it. For the first time in my academic career I made the Dean's list, which I maintained for six consecutive semesters in a row. How proud I was in 1992 to graduate *Magna Cum Laude* and walk in an Honors Ceremony to receive my Bachelor's Degree in Elementary Education.

George

"What was George doing here?" There were other things that confused my parents at the hospital and mom had to ask about them.

"George who?" I asked.

I had met George in October 1999 when I worked as a kitchen team volunteer on an evangelization retreat for young adults. George arrived at the retreat in a wheelchair. "Poor guy, how unfortunate." I had thought when I first saw him. I wondered what had happened to him. He arrived late the first evening and there was confusion among the leader and co-leaders as to whether he had actually paid or signed up for the retreat. To this day I do not know how it was resolved, but the director reluctantly agreed to his attendance.

On Saturday evening, after cleaning up from dinner, a group of us from the kitchen team chatted in the lobby. George was there. He talked with a few people I had come to know on the team. I learned that my friend Sarah and her husband Jonathan knew of him from his part time work at a Catholic bookstore. This reassured me he was an okay guy. So when he asked me to come to his home for a potluck and movie night he said he was organizing, I agreed. He asked me if I could contact people to come to his home. Basically he manipulated me to act as hostess for his party. Being fairly social, I invited ten guests that attended the gathering.

Thinking George might need some extra assistance, I arrived at his home a little early to drop off a pasta casserole and help set up for the potluck. He seemed agitated and distressed about something. I tried to calm him, assuring him everything would go just fine. People showed up, some ate and left, while others ate and stayed for the movie. It was a nice evening.

Before leaving with my girlfriend Theresa, he asked me to help him again, saying that he wanted to do this as a weekly thing. I was busy with work but said that I would help as much as I was able. Then George began to call often to remind me to help him with his movie nights. One day when I was unable to help him he got very angry with me on the phone. I thought he was just having a bad day.

George and I went to a few social functions together as friends but when he claimed involvement with gangs, occult practices and devil worship prior to his "christian" life I got the creeps and in January of 2000 I learned that the evangelical religious sisters at a local convent told him he was no longer permitted on their grounds I immediately ended our friendship. This was not an easy task. He got angry with me on the phone, his outbursts frightened me. This ultimately led me to end all contact with him. He eventually stopped calling me and left me alone. Because he was no longer a part of my life I didn't feel the need to tell my parents and worry them.

Because of my devotion and service in ministry, information about my accident flew threw the community like a bolt of lightening. There were many people at the hospital awaiting news of Nathaniel and my well-being. George called my parents' home late the evening of the accident telling them he had heard about the accident from some people. He requested information from my mom about what had happened and which hospital I was located at. My mother had no idea he was not a welcome part of my life. The next morning when my mother and father arrived at the Intensive Care Unit, George was at my bedside. My parents asked the staff how he got there and why he was at my bedside. The attending nurse told my parents he had claimed to be my brother.

I have no memory of George ever being in the Intensive Care Unit or what we talked about.

At the time my parents were desperately searching for information about what had occurred. Since George was next to my bedside talking to me, my parents assumed he was trying to help. It was not long after my release from the hospital that he was at our home every day bringing food and offering to drive me to doctor appointments. He was no longer in a wheel chair because he had experienced a "miraculous" healing.

When I reflect back on that time I can barely imagine the pain my poor parents endured. Not only was their daughter clinging to life at one hospital, their only grandchild was clinging to life in another. Back and forth they passed between the two hospitals. Unfortunately, at St. Joseph's Hospital they learned that my son's prognosis was much worse than mine. Nathaniel, the light of my life, for whom I would have given my life without a thought, had sustained life-threatening internal injuries.

My father, who had volunteered many years as a paramedic for the local ambulance department in our hometown in Pennsylvania, knew the procedure. My mom and dad, and friends Cindy and Michael were in the waiting room, eager for news of Nathaniel when the doctor arrived with two nurses by his side. When they entered the waiting room Dad immediately asked the doctor how Nathaniel was doing. The doctor said that he was required to speak to the parents first. My dad instinctively knew the dreadful routine. My ex-husband, Bill, Nathaniel's father, was waiting in the chapel with his cousin Phil.

My parents followed the doctor to the chapel with Cindy and Michael following behind them. My mother fumbled with a few words, gleaning, trying desperately to grasp for a sign of hope in the situation. One of the nurses reached out to compassionately hold my mother's hand as they walked. My mom began to cry out, "No! No! No!"

When they arrived at the chapel and gathered to hear the news, the doctor, who had tears in his eyes, told Bill and everyone present the terrible news. Nathaniel didn't make it. He had died. My mother described the cry that came from each person in the chapel that very moment as a loud wailing scream. When the brunt of this dreadful news hit my dad, he turned to the cross on the chapel wall and screamed to Jesus, "Why? Why did you have to take him from us? I hope you're happy that you have him with you. You have broken all our hearts!" When I learned of my dad's reaction later from my mom, I wanted to die because of the amount of pain I felt that my accident had caused everyone. I felt so responsible for the terrible situation and yet so confused by it all.

Time passed, though not very much before my parents rushed back to John C. Lincoln Hospital to see about my state. The injuries to my body were not life threatening. I had sustained a dislocated hip, fractures, bruises and cuts, but my parents' and the doctor's main concern was my erratic babbling and lack of coherence. It was decided that I needed to be attended to by professionals at a mental health facility. Before the doctors transferred me to St. Luke's Behavioral Center for further observation, they encouraged my father to tell me of Nathaniel's passing. They were concerned I might hear it from a nurse or a stranger. The doctors administered a tranquilizer. My dear dad's painful week was not yet over.

"Dawn?"

"Yes Dad?"

"We have something to tell you."

Deep down I knew something horrible had happened, but because of the lingering effect the prescribed narcotics had on me I was not coherent enough to understand the impact of it all.

"What is it Dad?"

"Nathaniel didn't make it in the car accident."

"What did you say Dad?"

"Nathaniel died."

Screaming on the inside, my reaction was flat outwardly. The medication was running its course.

Those were the last words I remember hearing before I sank into a dark abyss. Now the real nightmare began.

When the realization finally hit me that Nathaniel was dead and that it happened while I was taking care of him, I was incredibly angry at myself. I blamed myself, feeling deeply ashamed that I was not able to control my behavior and protect him from this horrible outcome. I did not understand the reaction I had experienced from taking this prescription medication having no idea what it was like to be in a psychotic state. I would equate it to what it might be like to be in a coma, but with your eyes wide open. I was aware that people and things were around me but I couldn't get to them. I couldn't communicate with them because my emotions and mind were paralyzed. If this weren't bad enough I heard frightening audible voices coming from out of nowhere. I wanted to run away from them but I couldn't, because I didn't know where they were coming from. And I saw things that weren't really there.

Something told me what was happening might or might not be real, but I was paralyzed, terrified and frightened and I couldn't get away. I had no power, no will, no control whatsoever.

After my father told me Nathaniel was dead and as the haze of the psychosis began to lift I wrestled with thoughts that there must be something terribly wrong with me. I had to fight daily, sometimes second by second, the temptation to believe God allowed this to happen because I was a bad person. Thankfully, my faith told me otherwise. I didn't have an answer as to why this happened, and I might not ever know, but I believed God's eternal nature was good and I refused to let those terrible feelings dominate who I knew I was in God's eyes—one of His children.

There are not many details I remember from the days immediately following Nathaniel's death. Those few things I do remember remain with me to this day. Something of importance I remember was Nathaniel's father, Bill, visiting me while I lay in the Intensive Care Unit. He extended to me a peace offering, sharing with me it was Nathaniel's fate, and his death was not my responsibility. Bill and I had had substantial differences that led to our divorce. I appreciated his words because I would need them dearly when dealing with the enormous guilt I felt over Nathaniel's death.

I spent four days at John C. Lincoln Hospital for the injuries I sustained to my body, and four days at St. Luke's Behavioral Center because, as Dr. Phillips stated in his records, I lacked the ability to reason clearly and my speech was not easily understood. During my stay at St. Luke's my parents had the daunting task of picking out a casket for their grandchild. Then they had to dress and drive me to my son's funeral.

The Funeral

The funeral took place at Saint Thomas the Byzantine Catholic Church in Gilbert, Arizona. This was the church where Nathaniel had been baptized and confirmed shortly after he was born. There are no words to adequately describe the pain I experienced while being driven to my own child's funeral. Feeling forlorn and forsaken I kept asking myself over and over again why an innocent and precious child was about to be hurled into a barren, gloomy and dark dirt ditch. Death had struck, it seemed, for no apparent reason. I was in shock. I felt as if I were entering an infernal labyrinth that twisted and turned without end. I could not make sense of anything. Much of what I share comes from statements given to me from family and friends as well as from my own limited pain-racked memories.

I arrived at the funeral with my parents. Because I had a dislocated hip and fractured left foot, my mother and father gently guided my steps while we walked to a seat at the front of the church. My parents sat on either side of me. Jennifer, a dear friend, lovingly led all in Rosary as her husband, Stephen, guided the congregation in meditation and song. Amidst the song and litany there lay the casket. Usually, the first thing I would see from this view was the gorgeous, hand carved Iconostasis and meticulously, vibrantly-colored, hand-painted icons of Mother Mary, Jesus and the saints. Placed on a table dressed in white lace, immovable and massive as Everest before me, laid my son's casket. From my feeble view, Nathaniel's casket seemed to take up every crevice of the room and in it lay the body of my sweet son.

At this moment the cry within me welled from so deep it frightened me. I never knew pain could be so terrible, so tangible. I thought I would die of heartbreak right there. If this had happened I would have been overjoyed, because it would have meant not one more moment lived without my son. Sadly, this would not be so. In that moment I could no longer hold in the pain. I screamed and cried from a place within me I never knew existed. My mother grabbed me in her arms and rocked me back and forth, trying to comfort me in my inconsolable sorrow. My friend, Theresa, said this moment stood out as a vivid memory for her. It made her think of the pain Mother Mary might have felt when Jesus died on the cross.

After a while I calmed down a bit and my mother lovingly encouraged me to go up to the casket to say my goodbye. This was a task no mother, no parent, should ever have to undertake, but a road that has been unfortunately taken by many before me.

Although Nathaniel lay only a few yards away, it appeared to me as the longest journey of my life. I stood up as steady and cautiously as I could. I took one timid step at a time in numbness and utter disbelief, fearing what I would see in the casket, knowing full well I was about to witness my worst nightmare come true. I grabbed onto the side of the casket with what strength I could muster and peered over the edge of its rim. I looked upon Nathaniel's precious body. What I saw shocked me. It was not the vivacious little breath of life that brought such joy and laughter into our lives, but a harshly bruised and badly swollen body. I knelt over to kiss Nathaniel's precious forehead, feeling more acutely the burden of his death as it weighed heavily upon my shoulders.

I remained a few moments more, and then slowly returned to the seat between my parents. I bargained with God in desperation, "Bring Nathaniel back to life. I know you can do it, I believe that you can. I'm begging you, please bring him back to life as you did Lazarus." I waited. I pleaded, hoping that my faith was as strong as a mustard seed. I begged and pleaded some more. Eventually I received my answer. **No.** It was deafening in its impact.

George had resurfaced when I was most vulnerable. I was in survival mode. George's angry outbursts and creepy behavior from the past were a distant memory compared to what I was dealing with at the present. I felt I had been dealt the worst blow a person could deal with. I wasn't thinking clearly; I couldn't imagine that on top of everything that had just happened that my life was in danger. But he was back, two months later, worming his way into my life again after he found out about my accident.

"And you yourself a sword will pierce..."
—Luke 2:35

Impossible as it may seem, I hold dearly to a comforting memory during Nathaniel's funeral mass. It happened during Jennifer's prayer of the Rosary. As I sat between my parents, and as the procession of people visiting Nathaniel's casket continued, I felt myself enveloped in a blanket of peace. I began to think of Jesus's mother Mary, and I realized there was someone out there who knew my pain. Then I imagined Mother Mary at the foot of the Cross, wearing black and the sky the same, as if a very bad storm had just passed through. There she stood, the Mother of God, with a longing I could barely put into words, looking upon the lifeless body of Jesus, hanging from the cross.

At this moment I seemed to better understand the Scripture passage from Luke 2:35, "and you yourself a sword will pierce."

I wondered if part of Mother Mary's pain and suffering at the cross, was not the intense longing to take the place of her son. Had she desired to bear His suffering as I myself wished it were me who bore my son's pain and death in the casket?

As my faith had taught me about this amazing woman, the Mother of God, her strength came not in arguing with the will of God, but surrendering to it. In this reflection I realized with all my life that I, too, must embrace the reality that my child was not coming back this side of heaven, and that I must, for Nathaniel's sake and the sake of my family, find joy in life once again. So I set out, being strong willed and minded, for the most difficult fight of my life, *my survival!*

A Letter Of Gratitude

To live means to love and to love means to live.
If I am going to truly live again after suffering this tragic loss
of the physical presence of my son Nathaniel Joseph
I must make an active choice to love again
despite the fear of suffering loss.

Nathaniel taught me an enormous amount
about what it meant to live life to its fullest.
To do anything short of this in my life
would negate the treasure
I was able to experience in seeing firsthand
this blessed world of ours through his eyes.

And so I would like to thank you for myself and for my family.
Those of you who offered the love and compassion of your hearts
through gifts given in presence, prayers, flowers and cards.
We are forever grateful.
Because it is through your gifts of faith ours was not shattered
and the light of life that has shown and shines
through Nathaniel's eyes continues to shine in our hearts!

If the love poured out to us by you is but a sampling
of the goodness that resides in men's hearts, we live in a
world that bears much hope for mankind and for its future.
Thank you again, we are forever grateful!

I wrote these words and placed them in a letter two weeks after Nathaniel's funeral. I sent it along with his picture to the hundreds of people who responded to Nathaniel's journey home.

Second Sorrow
Matthew 2:13

"Rise, take the child ... and flee!"

I wonder how confused Mary might have felt after the Magi left majestic gifts for her child and then being told shortly after this she must take the child and flee to Egypt because King Herod sought to destroy the life of her newborn Son.

Perhaps she thought something like this: *Was it not an angel that told me not to be afraid, that I would bear a Son of the Most High, and the Lord God would give Him the Throne of David?*[1] *Was Joseph not told by an angel not to be afraid but to take me, as wife into his home.*[2]

What an almost forgotten joy it was for me to hear my cousin Elizabeth's words, "Blessed is the fruit of your womb." Before I spoke a word Elizabeth knew his name, her Lord.[3]

How many names of the children and their mothers I will never know slaughtered by Herod's gruesome edict. I can barely stand to contemplate this. What awaits my Son?

I remember Isaiah: He was pierced for offenses, crushed for sins. What violence and contempt awaits him. My heart aches in this waiting...but I TRUST. I trust you my heavenly Father... I do not understand you but I trust in your will.

...and his mother kept all these things in her heart.[4]

Two

It Doesn't End Here

The days shortly after Nathaniel's death were heart wrenching and numbing. I was in a state of shock. I remember the mornings and the enormous void I felt, as if there were a gaping wound in the center of my chest. I would lie in bed thinking how I could possibly fathom a moment, a second, let alone a day into the future, because in it there was no Nathaniel. During these days, the only thing that got me through second by second and moment by moment was the thought I kept repeating to myself, "It doesn't end here. It doesn't end here. This life is only temporary. It doesn't end here."

"Thank God," I'd say to myself. "There will be a day I will hold my son once again in my arms because *it doesn't end here*."

It was not long after Nathaniel's death that the seeds of an idea for a Website memorial to celebrate his life sprang into my heart. This would eventually come about but not before my journeying into the hellish depths of anguish.

Home From The Hospital

The summer before Nathaniel died, I remember seeing a picture of a beautiful, bushy-brown-haired little boy in the newspaper. The headline above his picture stated, "Another Pool Drowning." In a fleeting moment, I immediately brushed away the horror, wondering if that ever happened to Nathaniel, could I survive? Now this battle lay before me.

Shock and intense loneliness pervaded my every moment. As I look back I thank God for the gift of numbness which kept the full brunt of reality from hitting me all at once. But the inevitable was due to happen with or without my desire. It was necessary for me to gradually face the reality of what had happened. But with most survivors of trauma the road back to recovery is not without its major pitfalls because trauma is messy business. For those who have been involved in the sudden and violent death of a child, studies show it can be the hardest of all traumas from which to recover. Instead of a gradual transition through the stages of grief to a life without my child, as if that were possible, much of the information I received in the aftermath of Nathaniel's death came to me in what felt like a full brunt body slam to my emotions.

After my arrival home from the hospital one of the earliest phone calls my folks received was from Bill. He told them of a phone call he received from an older gentleman he had known who recently came back from traffic school. This gentleman shared with Bill the footage he had seen during the class. He said they were using newsreels of Nathaniel and my accident as an educational tool. You could clearly see my face. He told Bill he thought that I should know this.

It as at this time I came to learn the tragic reality that my son was not in a car seat the day of the accident. This being unthinkable to me, I went numb for a moment, which immediately gave way to horror and information overload. I thought, "How in God's name can this be? I wouldn't drive Nathaniel across the street to the grocery store without putting him in a car seat! You are not serious. Please tell me that you're kidding with me and that this is all a cruel joke and a big mistake. There is no way this could possibly ever happen, just NO WAY!"

I wanted to scream with everything that was inside of me, but I knew if I let it out, I was going to scare everyone in the neighborhood, including myself. "Oh my God, oh my God, oh my God! This can't be true! This just can't be true...no, no, NO!" My dad shared with me that it was and he and my mom began the excruciating retelling of what happened the evening before Nathaniel's death. That was only the beginning of the painful learning process I would have to endure from the police and eye witnesses.

I learned that I drove Nathaniel from church to church and from town to town trying to save him from what I thought was "the devil." A friend who knew me well had seen my disposition at church that day, and being alarmed by my behavior she attempted to approach me. She said I had this wild look in my eyes and that I stared right through her as she moved to calm me as I held Nathaniel in my arms. She said I refused her attempts to talk to me and I ran away from her.

Another friend who also saw me that day later approached me, crying from guilt for not having done anything. She told me she could see something was drastically wrong. I assured her that she must forgive herself, that at that point there was nothing she could have done. I hugged her and thanked her very much for her concern. The genuineness of her empathy touched me deeply.

The Eye Of The Storm Hits Landfall

The barrage of painful learning continued as my parents were contacted by the reporting police sergeant who told them I must come to the police station for questioning. My dad arranged a time for us to go. Bringing in an attorney was not something I had even considered because I felt I had done nothing wrong. I would tell the truth as I had nothing to hide. The officer asked me a long list of questions as compassionately and directly as an officer of the law in this situation could do.

After his list of questions he asked me about the absence of a car seat. I responded that I didn't know why Nathaniel was not in a car seat because I was vigilant about placing him in one. I told him car seat safety was important to me. I had requested that both Bill and I have our own car seats in our cars. I wanted us to be assured the car seat was always safely secured because we did not have to buckle and unbuckle it by adjusting the straps too often. Then the sergeant asked where the car seat was and I began the retelling of what my mother and father witnessed of my personality change.

Nathaniel and I resided with my parents shortly after my divorce from Bill. My folks explained their observation of me a few days prior to Nathaniel's death as being one of fear and confusion. Normally a peaceful sleeper, my sleep pattern had changed. They remembered me being unusually suspicious and that Nathaniel was acting more restless than usual.

Nathaniel was an even-tempered child who would go to bed without a whimper. However, the day before the accident, Nathaniel demonstrated nervous body language and was very jumpy. The evening before, in the hopes of calming Nathaniel and helping him fall asleep, my dad made a reasonable and seemingly harmless decision to take the car seat from my car and put it in his SUV so he could play songs from a selection of Nathaniel's favorite CDs, which my dad kept in the middle console of his car. For what was Nathaniel's last drive with his grandpa, he and his "papa" listened to various songs as they drove around the neighborhood. When they played the CD Nathaniel began to calm down and drifted to sleep to the tune of Dean Martin's "Amore."

Unfortunately, back at the condo I was at the point of no return. The household readied for bed after Grandpa and Nathaniel's arrival back home. Grandma encouraged me to place Nathaniel in his crib, hoping that my nightly routine of singing him to sleep would resume. They told me that I placed him in bed and then nervously roved the kitchen and halls. My mother believed I did not get any sleep because throughout the night, off and on, I tried to crawl into bed with my parents as I murmured how they'd better watch out for Uncle John, who was visiting us from Pennsylvania, because he was "the devil."

That evening my parents tried to reason with me to go see my doctor the next day, thinking I might be in need of a medication adjustment for my thyroid. Mom said I got up and did laundry into the wee hours of the night because she heard the washer and dryer and saw meticulously folded laundry placed everywhere throughout the living room and kitchen.

Unfortunately for me, Nathaniel, and everybody else in the household, when morning eventually arrived, the voices and hallucinations had not ceased. After a wakeup cry from his crib, and in an instant before anyone had a chance to react, I had scooped Nathaniel out of his bed. My poor child was in an unchanged diaper and I was in the same clothes I had worn for several days. I left frantically without a purse or shoes for what I believed was an attempt to save my son's life. What little fractured memories I do have from this time are horrifying. My parents called several of my friends in the hopes that I had stopped there. The pieces began to come together as they discussed their own experiences and encounters with my recent behavior change, but they came too late.

Cindy and Michael were the first to receive the phone call that unleashed the torrent of dreadful news from the police department. For a long period of time the officers were unable to retrieve comprehensible information from me as they said I kept calling Nathaniel and myself by different names. Finally, after much effort, someone was able to retrieve a phone number for my friends, Cindy and Michael.

When Cindy and Michael received the police officer's call, they frantically passed the information to my parents. Everyone began to rush to the hospitals. My mother and father were told by the police sergeant that the back adult restraint in the car was clamped and the strap pulled out. Nobody knew exactly what happened that day but it was assumed I probably strapped Nathaniel in the back adult restraint of the car.

The sergeant asked me a few more questions and began to concentrate more aggressively on the issue of the car seat. Feeling that I had answered all questions to the best of my ability, I requested at that time to have an attorney. Thankfully, I did not have to seek one, because no charges were pressed.

In The Wake Of The Storm

A newsletter from Bereaved Parents of the USA, a national organization for those who have lost a child due to death, states: "We don't want to make a judgment on which kind of grief is more difficult, but sudden death is recognized as one of the most difficult to recover from because of the tremendous shock involved." It continues, "This shock affects the body as major surgery would."[1]

Right or wrong, I came back from the hospital to a home empty of any traces of Nathaniel's existence. My parents were managing their grief while running and maintaining a busy interior design business and thinking it would be better to remove all reminders of Nathaniel, took all of his things and put them in storage. I remember screaming, "I'm not ready yet! I'm not ready to let go of my son. I am not certain I ever will be." Nobody had given my parents a "How To" book that explains what to do and what not to do when a parent loses a child.

I came to learn in the days to follow how devastated my parents were. They shared with a friend that not only had they lost their only grandchild, but they witnessed their daughter in deep anguish. These trying days tested their faith and their spirits dramatically.

I remember one morning walking by my Nathaniel's room, thinking how sterile it looked. It once glowed with the bright colors of a Noah's Arc theme, his stuffed animals, footballs and basketballs and books about trains and tigers. The room that shouted "little boy's room" now regressed into its former ordinary self, a guest bedroom. He really wasn't coming home.

The vacant emptiness of Nathaniel's room challenged my faith and my identity as Nathaniel's mother. I ran to church to attend the sacrament of Reconciliation. "Father, forgive me, because I don't think I believe in Jesus anymore." He responded, "Dear child, the fact that you are even questioning the existence of God shows you have faith." His words consoled me deeply.

Whether I liked it or not, I was faced with a choice. I could allow myself to deteriorate, or begin the arduous task of rebuilding my life by rebuilding my shattered beliefs and self-confidence. I prayed by asking God for help, knowing that without Him I would surely die. A well meaning friend, well aware of my love for God, cried out in anguish, "How could God do this to you?" Not having any conceivable answer to this question or wanting to dare go down that line of thinking I yelled, "I need God now more than I ever have." Crying, I hung up on my dear friend who, in his own devastation, was trying to grasp the tragedy that was leveled against our family.

It took me several months after being released from the hospital to get behind the wheel of a car again. Actually, it was the wheel of a quarter-ton Dodge nine-seater van that my folks had just bought for their business. I remember feeling safer in the van than I did in a car. I believe it was the van that helped me regain my courage to get back out on the road again.

At this time of shock and sorrow I requested from my parents the names of the therapists they were given by the hospital upon my discharge. I called the first one on the list.

Dr. Martin was a wonderful, loving and patient therapist who listened compassionately to my pain and grief. He taught me relaxation techniques to calm the fear I had of once again losing my mind. He made a relaxation tape for me during one of our sessions and gave it to me to use at home. It was a wonderful meditation with visual imagery of a field and flowers, a waterway and trees. I used this tape often and found it very helpful along with my daily prayers.

I remember questioning Dr. Martin about my own sanity and asked him if I could be schizophrenic. He had extensive experience and more than a decade of tenure in a high-level mental health facility where he worked directly with schizophrenics. He assured me I was not schizophrenic. Hearing his reassurance brought me peace amidst my grief as I grappled with the havoc this prescription medication had wreaked in my life.

Lighthouse In The Storm

Thankfully, there were gracious friends who were unwilling to let me walk this path alone. I had met Rebecca several years before

Nathaniel was born, at a social gathering thrown by Cindy. Rebecca volunteered to drive me home after the event. We found we had a special connection. She was a rare find for a friend because she expressed a joy, peace and self-assured confidence that made her even more beautiful than she already was on the outside, if that were possible.

We kept in touch and talked for hours about our lives and struggles. We supported each other in laughter and encouragement by lifting each other up through difficult times. But Rebecca was out of the state visiting family when Nathaniel died.

I had settled in at home shortly after the accident when Rebecca paid me a visit and offered me a most precious gift. She asked if it would be okay for me to spend the next Friday evenings with her for as long as I needed. Out of generosity Rebecca chose one day a week where we met for many months amidst her busy schedule. I cried because I felt I had nothing to offer anyone and she chose a courageous path to walk with me during such a bleak time. I desperately needed an unconditional presence, and that was what she became for me.

In a way Rebecca was a "Simon" for me along my way of Calvary. Many times I would pour out my pain and she would listen for hours on those Friday evenings. She drove me to the park or a restaurant, or we went for a simple but life-giving walk around the block. She couldn't understand my pain—thankfully, she had never been through anything like it, but she chose a rare deed, to walk with me in my agony and lift me up when I was unable to see my way. How grateful I was for the months she took out of her life to be with me. I thanked her husband for lending me the gift of his precious wife and her time.

More Gracious Gifts

Another gracious gift came through a very important phone call I received from my friend Sarah, who shared with me news she thought might be helpful to me. It was about a ladies' prayer group at Saint Bernard of Clairveaux Church. She knew that I lived close to this church and heard that they were a wonderful group of ladies.

Sarah offered to take me and told me the time and location of the meeting. I recalled that I had spent quite a few times with Nathaniel in that very same room, which was the Children's Cry Room. The Cry Room is a place in the sanctuary with a large window that faces the altar. It is a child-friendly place where parents can sit together with their young children during mass instead of taking them to the church's childcare center. I thanked Sarah for her call, but thought to myself that I was not certain what I was going to do the next second let alone go to a prayer group with a group of ladies I did not know. I also felt I could not go into this room where I had once held my son.

I was grateful for Sarah's kindness but I did not go immediately. It wasn't until several weeks later that I thought maybe I should at least check it out. Eventually, I made plans to go, not knowing what to expect but hoping for the best. I decided to go to the 8:30 a.m. mass prior to the ladies' prayer group, because it always seemed to bring me peace and courage. I stayed a little while after mass sitting in the pew, not having much to say to God, just sitting there absorbing the surroundings and soaking in the solitude which seemed less threatening there than on the "outside." I noticed some ladies beginning to gather around the baptismal font which was in the back of the church, close to the Children's Room. I got myself up and began to walk in their direction.

As I passed by each one of them I noticed a peacefulness that resonated from their countenances, which put my heart at ease. When I entered the room I watched two ladies take out guitars from their cases and begin to tune them. I immediately realized what kind of prayer group this would be. Originally, I thought I had been invited to a bible study. It was odd, I thought, that Sarah would invite me to a praise and worship group. Praise and worship is meant to celebrate by singing joyful songs to the Lord. I was not feeling very joyful, and I was not sure what would come out of my mouth when they began to play.

Then, in a gesture of kindness, one of the ladies welcomed me and introduced herself. Her name was Laura and her friend was Ann Marie. I introduced myself and awkwardly began to tell her a little bit about why I was there and who had told me about the meeting. In a motherly way, Laura began to share a bit about the tragic loss of her own young son named Andrew. Saddened for her, I felt an immediate sense of connection and then relief that in this little room I might find some understanding. Little did I know this was only the beginning of many blessed encounters with this special group of ladies who would help to slowly walk me out of the valley of the shadow of death.

There were many gifts that came from this group, most importantly, the amazing courage, joy, fortitude and love these ladies exuded. I was surprised to learn that among the dozen or so women, six of them had suffered, along with me, the loss of a child. Each had their own tragic story, from losses through illness, overdose, and accidents, and each offered me hope as they modeled for me perseverance and trust. They walked with me, talked with me, cried and laughed with me. Most importantly they let me be me. These amazing women of God taught me the gift of how to praise God through my suffering. Over time I came to discover that in my weakness, residing within me was a mountain of strength. The roar of a lioness was born during this time and I learned that nothing was impossible with God.

Another amazing gift I received was when Laura shared with me a miracle of consolation she received while on pilgrimage to the mystical place called Medjugorje, where she journeyed with friends shortly after her son Andrew's death. While there, she stood on the mountain next to the cross that marked the site of the first reported apparition of the Queen of Peace. She sighed a prayer of longing to Jesus and His Mother Mary. She felt a deepening of peacefulness and with this the impression, "You will see your son again." She thought she might be going crazy but could not help but wonder what this might mean. She spent the next few days praying and resting in this sacred land.

When they came to the last day of their trip she became sad. She hoped she would receive a special grace to see her son. As she was coming down the mountain one last time, her friend, who had stepped into a little stand at the bottom of the hill, began yelling to Laura, "Come here! You have to see this!" Laura wondered what this could be about and rushed down to her friend.

When she got to the stand her friend took her by the hand and walked her over to the side wall where there were many 3-dimensional mementos of holy figurines displayed. Her friend asked her, "Look, and tell me what you see." Puzzled with her friend's enthusiasm, she began cautiously scanning the wall. All of a sudden her eyes fell upon one of the figurines that took the breath right out of her. It was a sculpted memento of the Blessed Mother Mary holding in her arms the child Jesus, but the replica of the figure of Jesus looked as if the artist had Andrew sitting right next to him as he created it.

Laura took in every detail and was amazed at the artist's representation down to the wavy curl in Andrew's bangs that Laura sometimes had to fuss with. This figurine had Andrew's cheeks, chin, eyes, nose, mouth and lips. Laura gladly purchased the memento from the store owner. At one of our meetings, she brought the memento for me to see along with a picture of Andrew. I was awestruck. The exactness in detail was undeniable, and I realized she received a beautiful grace of consolation and the joy of seeing Andrew again.

The Blessings Of Service

Another gift I received came by way of an invitation to serve on a young adult ministry retreat team, six months after the accident. How courageous the leaders of the team were to ask me to serve at such a time. It meant so much to me, as it provided a wonderful opportunity to be out of the house and spend time with friends. More importantly, it validated my personhood. Although tragedy had struck my life I still had a purpose. I gratefully accepted.

The first two meetings were spent getting reacquainted and meeting new people, praying and participating in ice breakers and sharing our lives together. At the third meeting, the retreat directors began the process of giving out our duties. Some of us would serve on the kitchen team and some of us would be small group leaders, while others of us would give talks on various topics that were applicable to the lives of the average young adult.

After prayer, the directors discussed each team leader's position. These were times of spiritual growth, because many times the duties assigned were not necessarily what we expected, but always ended up being what we needed to grow in faith, hope and love. The leaders went around the room giving out duties, and when they came to me I was asked to give a talk on the topic, "Faith in Action." They said that they felt my life was speaking loudly by my continuing openness to serve God through all my difficulties.

I was humbled and honored that the directors had chosen this important task for me. I knew almost immediately who I would talk about. As any parent who has lost a child knows, one of our greatest fears is that our child will be forgotten. This would be a wonderful time for me to be able to celebrate my son's life and encourage others in their faith walk.

The team began its three months preparation period and I believed this would give me ample time to prepare my talk. My preparation period turned more into a spiritual battle within me as I hung onto my faith for dear life while trying to avoid the chasm I felt in Nathaniel's absence. My faith journey spoke a language of its own. I call it my faith journey and not my grief journey, because I don't see the two as separate things, as I expressed in an email to my friend, Linda:

Hi Linda,

Let's put it this way, I will never be ready to give a talk about my life and walk with God in faith about this tragedy. Because of this I feel called to give it facing my current agony and wrestling match with God.

I pray that my talk will touch hearts in a way to show God is greater than our struggles and tragedies and that sometimes events happen in our lives that don't match up with our understanding of right and wrong. Faith is put to the test in a way not ever before challenged and intense soul searching is necessary to move forward in Christ.

Does this mean there are not going to be times of incredible anger and frustration? No, but whom better than God Himself can handle the kind of anger that stems from lack of understanding. Am I ever going to know why the Lord permitted my son to die in the way that he did? Maybe not in this lifetime.

This being the case then I have a choice to make, don't I? Is my faith based on having to have all the answers, or is it based on my belief that God exists and that He is a loving God and is always looking out for His children's well being. He could have permitted in a million ways for Nathaniel to still be here, but he is not, and why? Because God is a loving God and chose not to spare this blessed life for reasons greater than I will ever understand.

My talk will be based on the reality of where I am at in my present journey with God. Right now I am mad at Him, but I love Him and want to serve Him with all my heart. I believe God loves us so much He takes us where we are at and that all we have to do is simply say yes to Him.

To say that I am not mad at God right now would be a lie. I feel like what Jacob might have felt when He wrestled with the angel of the Lord in the desert. This angel in one fell swoop could have annihilated Jacob off the face of the earth. Especially since Jacob could be so rebellious. But God loved Jacob and knew his heart. He led Jacob into personal battle with Himself because he knew that is what Jacob needed, that it was in the struggle Jacob would grow more fully into who He called him to be, just as I hope He will do for me.

Linda, thank you for your love and support of me and for seeing something greater in me as I struggle to see it for myself right now.

God bless you,
Dawn Marie

Serving on the team, although challenging at times, enabled me to reacquaint myself with life. I began to drive again and took a part time job at one of the local five-star resorts as a pool side server. The job was tough on my back, but I welcomed the opportunity to be in such beautiful surroundings. I met many wonderful people and made a new friend named Kristi. We enjoyed eating lunch together and often shared our love for our faith.

"You may have to fight a battle more than once to win it."
—Margaret Thatcher

Still the gravity of my life situation amidst my continued efforts to press forward weighed heavily upon my heart. One day I received a crushing blow from a friend that about tore my heart to pieces. Strangely, I resisted returning her phone calls and finally gave into meeting her for a light lunch.

The conversation was awkward and uncomfortable, and her angry question upon our departure left me stunned and speechless. This was not a lunch that was meant to lift my spirits but an interrogation. As we readied ourselves to get up from the table she said in a demanding voice, "Why the hell didn't you put Nathaniel in a car seat?" My body trembled. I could barely speak, knowing that her words were the words of many, thanks to incomplete coverage by the media—and it was a question for which I simply had no answer. Although I believe she was speaking from a position of the fear dealing with her own child's mortality, I was devastated by her comment. This was a Saturday I would never forget.

Divine Encouragement

The Sunday following this shocking confrontation I was in emotional tatters. I went to church with my family. I could barely pay attention to the worship or the pastor. A swarm of thoughts besieged me: *You are never going to survive this. Even your "friends" think you're a sham. You don't deserve to be alive, look at all the terrible things you've done in your life. Your son is dead. It's all your fault…it's all your fault… it's all your fault!*

I could barely contain my sorrow and reached over to my dad and my mom. I told them that I was hurting and asked if they could say a prayer for me. They both smiled somberly and nodded their heads in affirmation. When the time came to receive Communion, we rose and began to make our way up the aisle to the altar. When I rounded the corner behind my father, I was overcome with deep peace and solace. I put my head down and I received inspiration. I imagined a very gray and misty background, looking as if the sun had just set and Jesus was in a desolate garden. He was slumped over a huge rock and was heaving deep breaths and a heavy sigh. I wished to console him but felt there was a lesson I needed to learn.

As I approached to receive Communion, I was overwhelmed with the scene impressed upon my heart. When I turned to walk back to my seat I felt a peaceful, still small voice: "You see my suffering my child. I, too, was betrayed. I, too, was mocked and abandoned. I, too, was not believed, even by those closest to me. I know your pain. I walk with you in yours."

When I sat again in the pew I cried quietly to myself. I felt the compassion of the Lord, that I was not alone and that He did not want me to carry this heavy burden which He had already suffered for at the Cross. Hopefulness returned to my heart and I was able to face another day.

My Herald

Then it came, on white parchment, while I was out to dinner with a friend at a Chinese restaurant that was around the corner from my home. It was there I received a herald, the cornerstone on which I built the means of surviving Nathaniel's death and the judgmental accusations that would be leveled against me and my family. My herald came by way of a fortune cookie. It read, "Keep On Charging The Enemy So Long As There Is Life." I taped its rousing message to the inside of my wallet. I read it often taking it to heart for purpose, direction and encouragement. Its lesson seemed timeless.

Wait And See

The retreat was a month away, and as a team we were approaching the weekend that was called "the overnighter." This was a time in which we went over last minute details and gave our talks in front of the core team for constructive critique before giving them to the larger young-adult community attending the weekend. As the overnighter drew near I seemed taunted by doubts and struggled to put my talk together. I considered dropping off the team.

My early morning prayer the Sunday before my talk went a little something like this: *Dear Lord, how in the world am I ever going to be able to give this talk? Who am I trying to kid here? It is only six months after my accident and I am giving a talk about faith in action. This is crazy. You would never ask me to do something like this so soon. I am tired of going back and forth on this, so I am going to make a decision. I am not going to do it.*

That very instant the phone rang. I wondered who could possibly be calling me that early on a Sunday morning. It was my friend Rich. He asked me what I was doing and I replied that I was praying. When he asked what I was praying about, I told him about not doing the retreat. He then asked a simple question, yet to me it meant so much more: "Why?" In the very moment he asked me that question the floodgate of tears began to flow and I realized my reason for not wanting to give my talk—FEAR, which I had heard many times referred to as "False Evidence Appearing Real." I quickly recalled the scripture 2 Timothy 1:7: "For God did not give you a spirit of cowardice, but rather of power and love and self-control." In that moment I said to myself, "I will be darned if I am going to let fear stand in the way."

Once again I heard my herald. "Keep on charging the enemy as long as there is life." I made the decision not to allow fear to get the better of me. I received some final words of encouragement from Rich. Before we hung up he said something to me of a prophetic nature, though neither of us knew it at the time. He said, "You're giving your yes to God. You wait and see the blessings that will come out of this!" Within the next two weeks I encountered a turn of events that would alter my life dramatically.

Finally, the overnight weekend had arrived. The directors and retreat team members gathered at the home of an older couple who were giving the Marriage Talk on the retreat. We would stay there Friday evening after work, sleep in bedrooms or sleeping bags, and finish by Saturday evening. This was a pleasant time, where those who were not on the kitchen team brought food for meals, snacks and drinks, giving the kitchen team a break from their contribution to previous meetings and the upcoming retreat.

Throughout the weekend we met and discussed last-minute preparations and details, putting finishing touches on the banner, typing words for the theme song, constructing name tags, etc. But the main portion of the weekend was spent listening to and critiquing the prepared talks. I had tried my best to put something down on paper, but all I brought with me was a picture of Nathaniel and me. When it came to my turn, not knowing exactly what I would say, I began to speak from my heart about my deep love for my son, my fond memories of being a mom, and the accident that changed our lives. In addition, I spoke about my personal faith journey and the pain I now endured, seeking purpose and solace from God in Nathaniel's tremendous absence.

Faith In Action Talk

I began with the scripture Luke 18:15–17

People were bringing even infants to him that he might touch them, and when the disciples saw this, they rebuked them.

Jesus, however, called the children to himself and said, "Let the children come to me and do not prevent them; for the kingdom of God belongs to such as these.

Amen, I say to you, whoever does not accept the kingdom of God like a child will not enter it."

I paused, — and then repeated:

Whoever does not accept the kingdom of God like a child will not enter it.

—What does this mean to you? I ask you to think about this for a moment.

On the table before you is a picture of a very special little boy. Okay, maybe I am being a little prejudiced, because he is my little boy. His name is Nathaniel Joseph and he taught me and continues to teach me what it means to have the faith like that of a little child. Nathaniel was born on November 10, 1997 and he went home to be with the Lord on March 18, 2000. I miss him dearly and would like to share with you a little bit about what I observed of his special love for and relationship with Jesus and Mary.

I will never forget the time when Nathaniel was only a few weeks old, at a time when a child's vision is still developing and they are more aware through the senses of sound and touch. I was sitting on the couch with my legs propped up on the coffee table with Nathaniel facing me in a sitting position on my lap. I was thoroughly captivated by this precious gift that God had blessed me with, taking in every minute detail of him. Nathaniel had a beautiful sweet face with big searching eyes that seemed to want to take all of me in, too. We gazed at each other in wonder as I sang to him. He was taken by the melodic sounds of my voice and we shared as any mother and father knows one of those sacred moments in each other's company. In a moment of love and prayer I said to my son, "Nathaniel, you know that Jesus loves you, Mary loves you and Joseph loves you." In the very instant I finished speaking my son smiled and spontaneously looked above my head to the left and sighed a quick "ah." Then, quickly, he pivoted his eyes to the center above my head and uttered another "ah," and then to the right above my head and uttered a final and distinct "ah." I had goose bumps, feeling I had just witnessed a small miracle of the presence of things unseen.

Nathaniel's Special Love For The Madonna

My talk continued with my memories of Nathaniel's special love for the Madonna:

Raising Nathaniel the short and blessed time I had with him was sweet and almost effortless at times, as his temperament was mild and easy going. When it was time to go to bed at night he would naturally and leisurely come to me to be enfolded in my arms. I would embrace him and take him to his crib for sleep. Our routine was quite similar every night as we entered his bedroom. I would hold him in my arms and sing a few bedtime songs to him. After about the third song he would drape his little head into the curve of my neck and I would hold him a few joyful moments more before placing him in his crib. Those sacred memories remain with me still.

One bedtime evening stands out particularly well as this was an evening in which Nathaniel's routine was unlike other times. It happened after a playful evening we spent with his grandparents. He had a full day at the park, swinging on the baby swing, sliding down the slide and making friends with a precious blonde-haired, blue-eyed little girl his age.

After he ate his dinner heartily and gave his grandparents a hug and kiss goodbye, Nathaniel and I watched a little "Brown Bear" video. When his eyes became droopy and he rested his head on my lap, I knew it was time for him to sleep. I picked him up to walk upstairs for our bedtime routine.

As I climbed the first steps, Nathaniel awakened in my arms and began to wiggle. When I reached the halfway mark of the climb on the stairs he began to wiggle even more. I wondered what he might want. Thinking he might need something to drink, I turned around and began my way down to the kitchen. As I neared the corner to enter the kitchen, Nathaniel began to squirm once again, but this time more dramatically. We passed the niche where I had recently placed a statue of the Blessed Mother. I stopped and walked over to the niche with Nathaniel in my arms, and he almost leaped out of them to lean over and kiss the Madonna right on the cheek.

He leaned back into my arms without a wiggle, his body completely relaxed. Then I realized THIS was what he wanted. I returned to the stairs, singing him a bedtime song, and then gently placed him in his crib with a smile and him in peaceful slumber.

It is amazing to me that in the short time I spent with my son I learned about having the faith of a child. How easily Nathaniel took things on faith, not trying to decipher or analyze, but through a simple and uncomplicated acceptance of Jesus and Mary he demonstrated his love for God.

I then spoke what I truly believed in my heart, of faith being a living, breathing organism that if not nourished, would surely die. I shared that the simple task of getting out of bed in the morning took faith for me after Nathaniel died and the only thing that got me out of bed was the repetitious phrase and firm belief that *it doesn't end here.* I spoke of the importance for me of prayer during this vital time, and what it meant to surround myself with people of lively faith such as the girls in the St. Bernard's prayer group. I spoke of how important it was for me to share my life with people who had journeyed this kind of loss before me and the encouragement they were for me to not remain stuck in my grief. It took faith for me to believe my suffering had meaning, and what a blessing it was for me when I reached outside of my pain to help another carry his or her burden.

I took the example of a bodybuilder and explained, as I lifted my arm up in an Arnold Schwarzenegger-like pose, the strength and bulging we see in the bicep comes from action. If we expect to build strength and shape to this muscle we have to pick up a weight and lift it, we have to eat the right kinds of foods and commit to an objective and stick to it. I shared that the same thing goes for our faith. If we do not nourish it, build it by reading Scripture, prayer, study and action, how can we ever suppose our faith will grow? Like a muscle, it will flop. It will surely struggle to expand and not become what it was meant to be.

The encouragement and positive feedback I received from the members of the group was amazing. I later read their critiques: *WOW!! I loved it.—Wonderful testimony!—Faith = Muscle, Great!—Become childlike to enter into the kingdom, Terrific!—Personalized information. Fantastic!—Your story is Powerful and will change hearts! Moving, Inspiring, Beautiful! From the Heart, the bottom of your heart, Very Awesome!—Personal, Outstanding! God Loves You!!!*

I could not thank everyone enough for their positive and generous feedback. It fortified me in my faith and instilled in me the gifts of courage, hope and love for the upcoming retreat weekend and the turn of events that were soon to follow.

I Am Not Alone

At 5:00 am on the Sunday morning following the Friday/Saturday overnighter, my mother gently woke me up. I perceived from her voice a sense of urgency. "Dawn sweetie, you need to get up and see this." *Oh,* I thought to myself, *What could this be that my mother would wake me up so early, knowing I just came from a busy two days*? Then she began to tell me about an article she had read in the newspaper. It was about a young man named Nicholas Jenkins who experienced a tragedy after taking the same medication I had been taking at the time Nathaniel died.

I began to read about another individual in another state whose family experienced severe trauma and loss just as mine had. The article talked about Nicholas slipping into a psychotic fog in January of 1999, just one year prior to our incident, believing "God" was telling him to leave his body and bring his daughter with him. The article told how he had shot his infant daughter and then himself in the abdomen with a shotgun. *How could he have survived?* I asked myself. This was incomprehensible to me; but survive he did.

When Nicholas recovered from the wound he was charged with murder. Psychiatrists testified before a judge that the shootings happened solely because of a psychotic state caused by prescribed medication. Brian Johnson, the Senior Vice-President of the pharmaceutical company that made the popular medication, said that this was the most severe case that had ever occurred. The judge agreed and ruled that Jenkins lacked the capacity to understand what he was doing.

Had I not been through the experience of Nathaniel's death while taking this same prescription medication, I would have read that article and probably thought, "Oh yeah sure, some nut case kills his kid and blames it on a drug." How terrible I now felt, thinking surely many people were saying this same thing about Nathaniel and me.

After reading the article I walked around in a daze for the rest of the day. Deeply saddened by what this family suffered, I was angry this had actually happened to somebody else, and only a little over one year before Nathaniel died. I did not know why at the time, but I felt I had to—I must—speak to this man. I needed to know if he went through the same experience I had. The article mentioned psychotic break. The next day I called information and gave them the name and city of the individual mentioned in the article. I was given a phone number. I dialed. The phone rang. A young man answered. It was Nicholas.

No Amount Of Money Will Bring Him Back

Immediately after Nathaniel's death, many well-intentioned people I encountered told me I should take legal action. I could not conceive of this. My immediate reaction when the subject came up was abhorrence. I actually thought to myself, *You are sick! How in God's name could you possibly be thinking about money at a time like this? That is the most disgusting thing I could ever think of. My child is dead and no amount of money is EVER going to bring him back.* I wanted to run away from these people.

I later realized their words stemmed from anger and fear. Some were angry that something so horrific could happen, as many knew the integrity and hard-working nature of my family. While others, I believe, feared that this could happen again and were faced with their own mortality or worse, the fear of losing their own child. Eventually, I came to a more compassionate understanding of their response, but at the time I thought it grossly insensitive.

Yet as time went on I tried to grasp for answers as to what it was that robbed me of my intellect, hitting me like a tornado, and ripping Nathaniel away from our existence. I searched endlessly in prayer, in conversations with family and friends, in books and in my own soul for a sense of meaning for the injustice of this terrible situation in which there seemed to be no answer.

Fear, anger and frustration pervaded many of my thoughts. Fear that a medication was capable of the power it unleashed in my life by altering so drastically my reality. Anger at the violent death my son suffered as a result of it. Frustration at having been stigmatized in the media and that individuals could be so heartless and uncaring to use video footage of the crash for "educational" purposes when they lacked the knowledge, empathy or desire to find the truth of the situation. Feeling at a loss, I considered and eventually contacted an attorney.

The attorney I contacted wanted me to take action against the doctor involved. When I realized this meant invading the business practice and possible private life of the doctor, by acquiring records and past history, it made me uncomfortable. It made no sense to me. Although the doctor probably had known that psychosis was a possibility that could happen, he was not under any obligation to tell me because the medication did not have a *black box* label.

The black box warning is the strongest notification given by the United States Food and Drug Administration (FDA) that a medication can carry as a warning of serious side effects and still be able to remain on the market. The black box is also sometimes called a *boxed warning* or *black label warning* because of the black border which surrounds the text that gives information about the exact nature of the warning. When a side effect is officially declared by the FDA, it will be found on the medication package insert labels as well as literature about the medication contained in advertisements in magazines. This prescription medication bore no such warning.

With a black box warning, doctors would be better alerted to educate their patients on the possibility of the occurrence of psychosis. Their patients could make a more informed decision about whether or not they wanted to take the medication, and if so, patients could share this information with their loved ones in order for them to watch for the potential warning signs of psychosis. In the case of children I felt this was especially important.

I later read the handout that came with the medication when I requested it from a local pharmacy. Psychosis was listed in miniscule print on the bottom of a one-inch-wide by two-and-a-half-feet-long handout. I was not given this handout by either the doctor or the pharmacist prior to the accident. I don't think I would have read every detail of it even if I did receive it because of its small print and extensive and sometimes confusing medical terminology. When considering my alternatives for pursuing a lawsuit I felt it would be inappropriate to take the doctor to court because he was not under obligation to tell me about such a deadly side effect as psychosis. But I truly wondered why this was the case.

Nicholas Jenkins and I talked for an hour. He shared with me a little about his family. He and his wife were the proud parents of three young children when they were blessed by a fourth. Tara was born over the Christmas Holiday in 1998. He was taking college classes in January of 1999 when he was prescribed the same medication that I was taking. Then he went into some detail about the nightmare of psychosis he had experienced and his infant Tara's death.

He described things that were familiar to me, such as having felt wired, flying high as a kite, racing thoughts and speech, and hearing frightening voices and commands. And then he said words equivalent to those I had said to others when I tried to describe the experience of psychosis: "It was like the gates of living hell opened up and swallowed me." As I had shared with many, "I should have been in a straight jacket, in a rubber room, letting that crap run itself out of my system."

As I spoke with Nicholas he told me a little about his attorneys. I decided to contact them for further information. I researched their Website and liked the work they were involved with. They were a small firm that primarily fought for the underdog. I appreciated that they helped an African-American woman with disabilities get her utilities turned back on. The first person I spoke with from the firm was James. I told him a little about what happened to Nathaniel and me and he told me about his partner, Peter, who would be in the area, and asked whether I would be open to speaking with him. I felt I needed to and so I said yes.

The Toughest Thing You'll Ever Do

Since I had no idea what to expect from them or myself, I was nervous the day I was to meet one of Nicholas's attorneys. As Peter walked up the aisle at the airport to greet my mother and me, I thought I was meeting Crocodile Dundee. His casual attire and laid-back appearance immediately put me at ease. We met in a little conference room at the airport and had a brief discussion about Nicholas's case. Then we discussed what happened in my situation.

While at the airport I told Peter I could not do this for money. Peter was polite about this but direct. He gave me some information to take home and read. He made the suggestion that I take some time to think and pray about the situation, saying that should I decide to proceed, it would be the toughest thing I would ever do, next to losing my son. His comment to pray struck me as odd coming from an attorney. I was not sure at the time why, yet I felt comforted by his mentioning this, because prayer was my lifeline.

The toughest thing I would ever do. How could that be possible? Nathaniel was dead. However, I would come to know the truth of his words. Yet, I needed something tangible in the way of change for me to seriously consider taking on this battle. I was infuriated about what had happened to my son. I felt this medication was a serious threat to the public.

I took the information home that Peter gave me and for the next few days I read it over. I wish I could say that like the saints I prayed about my decision or like Mary that an angel appeared to me and told me what I should do, but it was more like anger and disgust that pressed in on my emotions. I read about greed, neglect and irresponsibility. Had things been handled better another child might be alive today. I discussed this briefly with my family but I already knew what I was going to do.

The weekend I spent reading about Nicholas's case my blood began to boil. I learned that the then vice president of marketing for the pharmaceutical company said they had always been aware there was a risk of psychotic side effects with their prescription medication! In addition, the VP mentioned that during clinical trials of the drug there were reported instances of psychosis. *Then why*, I thought to myself, *is the mention of psychosis on the bottom of a two and a half foot-long handout in microscopic print? Wasn't psychosis a more hazardous side effect than dry mouth or constipation!* Finally, when I learned that the foreign-owned company did not sell this drug in its own country, I became angry.

More accurately, it was as if a fire was set ablaze in the center of my soul. I became disgusted at the hypocrisy of the situation and seriously wondered, if someone else knew then, what I knew now, would I want them to tell me? With the answer to this question, I had my decision as to whether or not I would take this battle on. Yes! I took up arms, the largest fight of my life next to losing my son, because I could not, would not, tolerate the tragic reality that my son was collateral damage!

Be sober and vigilant. Your opponent the devil is prowling around like a roaring lion looking for [someone] to devour.
—1 PETER 5:10

The pain I experienced in seeing young children with their parents was inexplicable. The guilt I felt in the wake of Nathaniel's absence was unbearable. It was as if his death had literally crushed everything inside me. I often wondered whether I would ever see the light of day again. The tunnel I looked down appeared very long, very dark and very endless.

Words Of Consolation

One day in June of 2000 I sat down with a pen and paper. I love to write letters to family and friends. On this particular day I intended to write a letter to Nathaniel. I didn't get very far. It ended at my first sentence—being a letter to Nathaniel, that is. It turned out to be a letter to *me*.

Do not be sad for me my mother. I am at peace and my prayer for you is that you, too, be at peace for the unfortunate circumstances in which you now find yourself. Mother, the accident was not your fault. I know that it was not, nor ever could be your intention that I die or experience death in that way. We are all going to die some day, Mom. It was just that Our Heavenly Father willed my entrance into Heaven before you. But do not be saddened or hurt, because Our Heavenly Father loves you as much as me. It is not because He loves you less that you must walk your present journey separated from me—physically that is, only physically are we separated, because I am with you now in a way more present to you than I was when on earth.

Nathaniel's tender words of love touched and consoled me deeply that day, and how true I found this statement to be of his presence.

Third Sorrow
Luke 2:48

"They journeyed...but did not find him"

I wonder what dread and apprehension struck Mary when she searched amongst relatives in the caravan and discovered Jesus was not among them. It was customary every year for the Jewish people to travel to Jerusalem to celebrate the feast of Passover. What was joy for Mary might have turned to fear when Jesus was not found.

Perhaps she worried, *Where could He possibly be? I've looked everywhere and for three days no one has seen him. He is only a boy. I wonder if he is frightened or alone? Has he eaten or had anything to drink?*

Upon Him was the chastisement...by his stripes we were healed.[1] *Is He in harm's way? Could it be my fault he is nowhere to be found? Did I lose my precious son?* Out of the depths have I cried unto you, O Lord. Lord, hear my voice.[2]

Oh dear, the sword. Simeon never foretold how or when. Will I ever see my precious Son again?

Finally! He is found, in the temple. And all who heard him were astounded at his understanding and his answers![3]

His words to me, His being about His Father's business.

Have I really found Him?

...but I TRUST. I trust you my heavenly Father...I do not understand you but I trust in your will.

...and his mother kept all these things in her heart.[4]

THREE

A MOM'S SEARCH FOR MEANING

WE READ IN THE BIBLE that the Mother of God and her husband Joseph lost Jesus after having celebrated the Feast of Passover in Jerusalem. Three days they searched for him among the caravan. The experience of losing something precious and invaluable touched their frightened and bewildered hearts. They found him. Eventually their joy returned.

I, too, knew the experience of having lost something precious and valuable beyond measure, in addition to losing Nathaniel. I experienced the loss of innocence and trust in God when my godfather committed an unconscionable, self-serving act of violence against me. He sexually abused me. My broken heart and shattered faith would lead me to some destructive choices in adolescence and young adulthood.

The assault happened one Saturday morning, when I was twelve. I was fulfilling my weekend chore of cleaning our home and had no way of knowing that asking my godfather's assistance to fix a pilot light that had gone out in our dryer downstairs was a catalyst for assault. By pretending he didn't know where the laundry room or dryer was located he tricked me into leading him to the corner of the laundry room. (He had lived next door to us for years and knew very well the layout of our home.) I had to turn away from him to show him where the problem with the dryer was. When my back was turned he attacked me from behind by groping my breast. Terrified, I fought off his attack. I grabbed his hands from my breast and shoved him away. Frightened for my life, I pushed past him and ran as fast as I could upstairs to my bedroom. He was right behind me. I slammed my door shut before he could enter and quickly locked it. I trembled and nervously paced back and forth in my room, not knowing what to do. My body shook as if a tremor of an earthquake had just hit and I felt like I might be swallowed up by the ground crumbling beneath me.

My parents weren't going to be home for hours because they were at work. I didn't have a telephone in my room. I felt the horrible suffocating feeling of being trapped. I had no way out. I stayed in my bedroom for what seemed an eternity not daring to unlock my door.

It could have been minutes, it could have been hours. All I know is that when I finally mustered the courage to leave my room he was standing at the top of the stairs. It was at this point I had a decision to make. I decided not to run this time but stay and somehow gathered within me the courage to look him in the face and conveyed to him, "You'd better not mess with me." He left, but not before warning me to keep my mouth shut.

My developing faith in God was shaken to its core. A godparent was supposed to oversee the child's spiritual growth in the Catholic faith, should something ever happen to the parents' ability to do so. I didn't tell a soul at first because I feared that no one would believe me. He was a successful manager at a major department store. I was just a kid.

In his book *The Wounded Heart,* Dr. Dan B. Allender gives an explanation of the dynamics that can happen in a situation like this. He says, "The moment core trust is lost in a relationship, efforts to understand and nourish the other person are forgotten in a battle to control and minimize damage to oneself."[1]

I was a prime example of Dr. Allender's words. After several months of trying to reach out for help, crying out to my mother, screaming my pain over my godfather's actions, she stood frozen before me without a reaction. She said nothing and did nothing. I felt as if I had just screamed my guts out in vain to a cement wall. Still I held onto a glimmer of hope thinking that surely she would tell my dad and he would do something. I waited and waited and waited and he too did nothing to defend or protect me. At the time I was too confused as to what I should do or to whom I could turn. (I later learned that my mom never told my dad until I was much older.) I began to think I was dirt and blamed myself for my godfather's attack against me. To try and deaden the pain I experimented with alcohol. I hung out with the wrong crowd. Shortly out of high school I became sexually active. From here things went from bad to worse.

After I finished one year of college, my parents decided that we would move to Arizona. I thought this would be a great avenue for a new start. The only problem was my mom and aunt were in business together and the abuser's family decided to come as well. It felt like a nightmare from which I couldn't escape. So with my fresh start came my old behaviors.

We arrived in Arizona on my twentieth birthday. I immediately entered the club scene. I met the person who I thought was "the man of my dreams." You know, "the one" who would solve all my problems and take away all my pain. Unfortunately, we never gave our budding friendship a chance to mature because we immediately entered into a sexual relationship which led to my getting pregnant.

Because his focus was school, having a baby was not an option for him. Going to my parents, as I learned from the past, wasn't an option either, and so I acted against my conscience and chose death over life. I drove with my boyfriend to a clinic that provided abortions. This decision had a horrible affect on me. My boyfriend told me that after the abortion I went from vivacious to solemn. I believe Mother Theresa's words when she said there are two deaths in every abortion—the child and the conscience of the mother. It was a tragic decision we both had made.

Mercy Abounds

I have come to believe, through several answered prayers, that my baby was a girl. Her name is Faith. After Faith died, so did a very big part of me. My relationship with her father began to self destruct. One evening in July of 1988, when our paths crossed at a night club, he indirectly became a catalyst for my conversion. He spoke cruel words to me that hurt me deeply. A little while after he left, something extraordinary happened to me. In the middle of the noise of this dance club I was surrounded by an indescribable sense of tranquility and calm and then, just as if out of nowhere, I was immersed in a light and felt as if someone had turned on a set of eighteen-wheeler high beams in the center of my soul. The Hound from Heaven had arrived whether I was looking for Him or not.

I began to think to myself, "What am I doing with my life?" I looked around at the glitz of this Scottsdale nightclub and asked myself, "Why am I here?" I walked out of the club that evening, leaving my girlfriends behind. I began to drive and drive and drive, when another thought popped into my mind: Saint Maria Goretti Church.

I had fallen away from the church for a period of time. I had recently heard someone say that Saint Maria Goretti was a pretty good church. I arrived there around midnight. I pulled into the dark parking lot and found a parking space near the front entrance of the church. It was mystical looking, with unique architecture that was in the shape of a tent that resembled what the Israelites had used long ago.

I pulled into the spot and sat there, when in the silence something deep welled up from within me. I know it now to be the Holy Spirit, but at the time I had no idea what it was, or better said, who He was. I burst into tears. I cried, "Why God, why? What on earth am I here for? This life is a joke. It's nothing but pain and sadness, betrayal and backstabbing. And my life God, I've made a mess of it. I beg you dear God if this is what life is about, I don't want it anymore." With tears and flushed face I cried, "Please take it!"

In that moment I knew He did. I felt saturated in the most indescribable love and peace beyond anything I had experienced before.

Shortly after this, my life flashed before me as if in a movie and I saw all the areas of my life in which I had hurt Him, Our Lord. Instead of feeling judgment or condemnation, I felt His love and mercy cover every hurt and pain I had caused Him. I cried from an even deeper part of me that I had ever known existed.

This time my tears meant reverence and awe for this Merciful God who I knew loved me to the depths of my being. I cried for quite a while in this state of grief and comfort, grief over my sins and comfort in the arms of His Mercy. As Our Lord told St. Faustina, "The graces of My Mercy are drawn by means of one vessel only, and that is trust. The more a soul trusts, the more it will receive."[2]

I began to trust again the God of my early childhood. The next day I ran as fast as I could to find a priest for the Sacrament of Reconciliation. I poured my heart out to him and left with an even deeper sense of God's peace and love for me.

> *Putting away falsehood, speak the truth, each one to his neighbor, for we are members of one another. Be angry but do not sin; do not let the sun set on your anger, and do not leave room for the devil. (25–27) And do not grieve the holy Spirit of God, with which you were sealed for the day of redemption. All bitterness, fury, anger, shouting, and reviling must be removed from you, along with all malice. [And] be kind to one another, compassionate, forgiving one another as God has forgiven you in Christ.*
>
> —Ephesians 4:30–32

I felt strongly that with the gift I had been given, I, too, must give back, and so I decided to extend the offer of forgiveness to the perpetrator of my childhood abuse. His reception of my confrontation was ill received as he began to mumble and deny his actions. I immediately told him to be quiet and listen to what I had to say. I told him that what he did was a terrible thing and that his behavior was horribly wrong, but that I forgave him for his assault against me as a child, and I prayed that he himself seek forgiveness and mercy from God, that he might one day get to Heaven. I have since come to learn important lessons on the myths and truths of confrontation of an abuser in a dangerous situation like this.

Forgiving my mom had been a much harder task because she was the more permanent person in my life. Yet according to a dear friend, Father David, since I made the decision in my heart to forgive her, even if my feelings told me otherwise, I had still granted her forgiveness. An immeasurable aid for me in the release of bitterness and anger was the Forgiveness Prayer from the wonderful book titled *Miracle Hour* by Linda Schubert. As Jesus said to his disciples when they questioned their failed attempts to unbind a young man from a deaf and mute spirit, "This kind can only come out through prayer." (Mark 9:29)

And here I would like to I say, if a person has been hurt or is hurting and in need of sincere confession find a priest, search for one who will listen to you with his heart. It is his duty, and if he has no time, as many are exhausted and overworked, and some struggle with selfishness just like the rest of us, then find another until one will listen. Do not give up on the desire to experience the Sacrament of Reconciliation which is a permanent sign that will recycle and renew a soul. As a good friend told me: "Do not let fear kick you in the butt; you kick fear in the butt."

With my new enthusiasm I began to discover the richness of the Catholic faith of my youth. It was also at this time I began to develop a hunger for the Word of God and the Holy Eucharist. I began to read with impassioned enthusiasm the lives of the Saints. My favorite became and remains Padre Pio of Pietrelcina. I will never forget the day I was introduced to him in September of 1988. Someone had lent me a video of his life called "Pray, Hope and Don't Worry." After watching it, I remember being flabbergasted that he actually existed during my lifetime. I was even more stunned that in all my years of being Catholic, I had never heard of him until that day when I was in my early twenties.

Padre Pio was born Francesco Forgione to Grazio and Maria Giuseppa Forgione on May 25, 1887, in Pietrelcina, Italy. He lived a simple peasant life although his spirituality was extraordinary, and at the age of 15 he entered the Capuchin Friars in Morcone, Italy. It was here that he received the Franciscan habit and was given the name Brother Pio. On August 10, 1910, at the young age of 23, Brother Pio was ordained a Catholic priest in the Cathedral of Benevento, Italy. In September 1916, he was assigned to Our Lady of Grace Monastery in San Giovanni Rotondo, Italy, where he would live for the rest of his life.

On August 5, 1918, he experienced the transverberation of his heart which caused a visible wound on his side. Then on September 20, 1918, he would receive that for which he would come to be known around the world, the stigmata, where his hands, feet and side were pierced with the nail marks and the lance wound of our Crucified Lord and Savior. He became the first Catholic priest ever to receive this grace. With this suffering came a notoriety he would rather happily have endured unnoticed. In his lifetime he would be visited by hundreds of thousands of people from every part of the globe, who sought him out for his spiritual direction and prayers. It was estimated by doctors that for the 50 years following the reception of the stigmata, he lost a cup of blood every single day.[3]

How joyful I was to discover in Padre Pio a strong and loving Father figure who cherished his "spiritual" children, one of whom I soon officially became, my name being listed in the directory in Our Lady of Grace Church in San Giovanni Rotondo. For Padre Pio stated that never shall he cease to rest until all his spiritual children have entered the gates of heaven.

I studied and learned as much as I could about this amazing figure. He had been granted, through efficacious union with God, the gifts of bi-location, perfume, language and of reading your soul. But the things I appreciated and adored most in this great saint were his no-holds-barred view and devotion of God and Mother Mary, and his deep love for the humanity he had sacrificed and suffered so much for and of their salvation.

"Mishaps are like knives, they either serve us or cut us, as we grasp them by the blade or the handle."
—Herman Melville

I remember my initial reaction to learning about the origin of this prescription medication and its ugly side effect of psychosis, and about how it contributed to Nicholas and his family's tragedy. I told Peter and James that I wanted this drug off the market! I felt the public had a right to know. This is when Peter shared the unlikeliness of one person being able to do this, but that through the suit we could raise enough awareness of the complications and questionable history of this drug and its maker to possibly put enough pressure on the FDA to "black box" the medication. I felt this was a reasonable and positive step in the right direction.

Here it was, two weekends before the retreat, and I had filed a lawsuit against a multi-billion-dollar corporation. My focus had been temporarily redirected. I resumed my presence of heart and mind and marched forward, trying not to allow the new challenge to take me from my present course. I was determined to focus on giving my part-time job my best and give the best darn faith-in-action talk those attending the retreat had ever heard. Then something out of the ordinary happened.

The week before the retreat I received an unexpected voicemail on my phone. It was a message from Christine Taylor, a producer from a major news network, who wanted to talk to me. I wondered what this could be about and so I called her. She told me that she had heard of my tragedy and that she was in California, on her way to New York. She said she could stop in Arizona before going back to the East Coast if I would be open to talking with her about Nathaniel and our unfortunate circumstances. I told her that I would be unable to meet her over the weekend because I was working on a retreat team. We scheduled the meeting for the Monday after the retreat.

After I hung up with Christine I was a ball of emotions. What if the network decided to do our story and I lost control and fell apart on camera from the pain I felt? What if they did the story and people judged me and rejected what I had to share with them? However, as I had always been more inclined to deal with the fear and move forward and do what needed to be done, that is what I intended to do.

Still, being only human, I worried that my feelings of apprehension would redirect my focus from the upcoming retreat. I called several friends, seeking encouragement, and asked them for prayer. Many of my friends prayed. When I called my girlfriend Rebecca, who generously spent those many Friday evenings with me after the accident, I got her answering machine. I left her a message, asking her if she could call me when she was available because I had something important to tell her.

It was early evening when Rebecca returned my call and I sensed heightened emotion in her voice. I thought it was because I told her of the importance of my call. She immediately asked me what was going on. I shared with Rebecca the conversation I had had, but before I could get Christine's last name out of my mouth Rebecca shouted "Taylor!" "Yes," I said, thinking to myself, how in the world did she know what I was going to say? Then Rebecca said, "Christine Taylor is one of my best friends from high school. I haven't seen her in eleven years. She called me from California saying she was on her way to New York stopping in Arizona to do an interview and asked if we could get together for coffee!"

"Wow," we both said, since Rebecca was raised in Oregon and I was raised in Pennsylvania. My apprehension immediately went away. I felt peaceful that Monday evening's meeting was in God's hands and not mine.

Christine and I had arranged to meet at a local restaurant for our Monday evening appointment. I was joined by my mother and my father, and at my invitation Rebecca came, too. Christine was what is called a mini-producer. This means it was her job to put feelers out to see if a story is newsworthy. My mother, father and I painfully shared a little about the day before and after Nathaniel and I had the accident. After she asked a few more questions we moved on to talking about the weather. I remember thinking that the appointment was not what I had expected because of its brevity. Still, I felt peaceful, and believed it was a step in the right direction toward getting to the public what I felt was important information.

Waiting to hear whether or not our story was "newsworthy" was a painful process. Months went by, which felt more like years, and I'd heard nothing as to whether or not our story was going to be told. I had given up all hope when, in late July, I received a phone call from another producer. This young woman was higher in the ranks. She asked a few questions and very soon my parents and I had made arrangements to meet her the following week. She came to Arizona where once again we met at a restaurant. This producer asked more in-depth questions than Christine Taylor had. When she was finished, she asked us about our willingness to retell our story to the public. My parents and I had already spoken in depth about this possibility and we told her that we would agree. Within a few days, a camera crew arrived along with one of the news anchors from the show.

The Pain Of Retelling

The news network reporter interviewed all three of us. At one time we were interviewed together, but mostly we were interviewed separately in different locations. It was an extremely difficult process to recall and retell the terrible day once again. Seeing my parents' anguish resurface made me want to tell everyone to go home in order to ease their pain, yet I barely endured the process of expressing my own grief and heartbreak. I continued by reminding myself why I was putting myself "out there." Would I have wanted to know this information beforehand in order to have made a more informed decision on the care I was receiving? My answer being yes, I pushed forward.

Taping the segment took two days during a weekend. When the camera crews and reporter completed their task, they packed up their equipment and flew back to their headquarters. As quickly as they had come, they were gone. Once again I was in a process of waiting. I was told they would contact us to let us know how soon the program would air.

The World Turns Upside Down

On that fateful eleventh morning in September of 2001, my alarm clock went off and the radio host announced that a plane had hit one of the twin towers in New York City. Alarmed, I thought it might have been a small plane like a Cessna. I yelled down to my parents who were making breakfast at the time to turn the television on quickly, because something dreadful had happened. Then I ran downstairs to see what was happening.

As we watched a burning tower I will never forget what we witnessed next. I remember my father exclaiming, "There is a second plane, there is a second plane!" Mom and I, still reeling with emotion from seeing the first tower ablaze, had not noticed it. Then it hit. We all stood there shocked and motionless, just staring at the television as now both towers were ablaze.

We watched in dread and pain for all those involved as the buildings eventually collapsed in on themselves. *This is America*, I thought. *How could this be happening?* The news continued. There were more planes involved. The Pentagon was hit. How surreal it all felt. Here I was, seeing terrorism on my country's own turf, while relating in an unsettling way as the events unfolded before my eyes. I felt that I, myself, had also experienced terrorism, but mine happened on the turf of my own heart and mind.

I was working as a preschool aid at the time of the 9/11 attacks. I will never forget the nervous behavior of our preschoolers. It was obvious the children knew something terrible had happened. Many of them had an unusually difficult time following directions. There were more "potty" accidents that day, more outbursts and more clinging that all the teachers noticed.

Reserved little Sarah was unusually talkative, and asked so many questions we couldn't keep up with her. Brian, usually timid and compliant, got out of circle and station time too often to count. Steven, who liked to work by himself, needed constant help and attention throughout the day. When Missy, usually the first out on the playground without looking back, asked to hold the teacher's hand at recess, lunch and again in the afternoon, we knew the day had affected all of them.

Even the teachers were clinging to schedules and calls from home for some sort of stability and sanity during the day. But I could not help but wonder if some of what I noticed in the preschoolers' nervous and unusual behavior was not also what my parents saw in my own son's behavior the evening preceding that fateful March day.

Shortly after the air strikes on United States soil I received a phone call that the network was ready to air its program, and it was only two months away. I had mixed feelings about this at the time. The air date was to be only two days before my son's birthday in November and here it was that our country was in the middle of trying to deal with and heal from its own "D-Day." How downhearted I felt that my story was to air so close to all the devastating loss that happened on September 11th. Still, I believed with all my heart that my story needed to be told. I was just unsure about the timing of it all.

The Show Airs

The national news program centered on the pros and cons of using medication to treat the controversial diagnoses of attention deficit disorder and attention deficit hyperactivity disorder. Its focus was not strictly on the tragedy that Nicholas and I shared; nor did it set out to condemn persons for choosing the route of medication to treat ADD and ADHD, as they also interviewed a family—a mother and her two son's—all taking this same prescription medication, and who all claimed they benefitted from the drug. But it helped to raise questions as to whether solely using medication for these disorders was always prudent, and it also tackled the issue of potential abuse of these powerful medications.

The show began by taking the cases of two little boys who had been diagnosed with ADHD. It discussed these sets of parents' intense struggle to help their sometimes abrasive children. One set of parents had gone the route of medication while the other, already having tried it without success, went the route of therapy and nutrition.

The show also focused on the fact that it was not only children who were taking these medications. It talked about several adults who experienced struggles with them, which included our stories. When the reporter asked me what my experience was like when I was taking this prescription medication, I told her that I knew what it was like to have been insane. I also said to her that the best thing for me that day would have been to be in a rubber room in a straight jacket. As I look back at this statement I could not agree more with what I had said. I was out of control and a danger to society, my child and myself.

But on March 18, 2000, I was not in a rubber room but behind the wheel of a car in a psychotic state. I shared with the reporter that it felt like hell inside of my mind and that I could not stop myself. The voices in my head had me convinced Nathaniel had been cursed, and that he would die if I didn't get him to a church. The show explained how I had no idea at the time, but now I believed my psychosis was a reaction to this medication which was prescribed to treat my attention deficit disorder.

To this day I am not certain, nor will I probably ever be certain, as to what actually happened that day Nathaniel and I crashed in the car. I believe this is more likely a grace from God, because to have seen the aftermath, of which I have no recall, I probably would not have survived the memory of seeing my son's badly injured and broken body.

The program impartially mentioned that I had previously been hospitalized for depression about a decade before but that I had no history of psychosis. As it continued, my dad shared his heart, saying that the person who was in that car that day was not Dawn Marie. The reporter asked my parents whether they blamed me for what happened. In unison my parents exclaimed, "Absolutely not!" My dad continued by saying the bottom line was that if I wasn't on that medication this wouldn't have happened.

The story continued that because I had struggled in my undergraduate work I had wanted to make sure that I would be able to focus on my studies this time around. I described some of my struggles with concentration in college. I was asked if my experience while taking this prescribed medication was positive. Trying to make my point, I stated with firm sarcasm, oh sure it was positive, if you liked flying like a kite. Looking back, I remembered how terrifying it had felt while taking this prescribed medication, the ceaseless rush of lofty emotions that mimicked a false "high" that never let up. The story continued with coverage of how I began to turn on my family. My mom mentioned their fear that I was having a nervous breakdown.

My parents explained that when they noticed Nathaniel acting unlike himself, they looked at each other and said that something was wrong with Dawn Marie. The show reported that my parents were unaware of my taking the prescribed medication. My dad reported how he pleaded with me to go to the doctor the next day. He said I had agreed.

However, when the morning arrived I grabbed Nathaniel and took the fateful drive. I expressed my deepest anguish that I never had the chance to hear my son say, "I love you Mom." He was a typical boy who preferred playing to talking. He was just beginning to give words form and put them together into sentences. I then shared the guilt I now carried for having ever taken that medication in the first place. I expressed how that was my biggest cross.

A segment of Nicholas Jenkins's story was also told. Nicholas bravely recounted the tragic day of his loss. Nicholas commented how he had no inkling or ability to say what was wrong with him, that the capacity to explain this was not there at all.

The show discussed my pain and anger at finding out from my mom that there had been a similar incident just a year earlier. The reporter shared how both Nicholas and I were completely unaware that psychosis was a possible side effect. She unraveled a one-inch by two-and-a-half foot package insert, considered adequate by the FDA. She said the insert listed psychotic episodes, and rare, under the central nervous systems adverse reactions section. Nicholas restated that he was not informed of this by the doctor, or given any other information.

The reporter asked me to pretend she was a representative from the pharmaceutical company sitting with me right then. What would I say to her? I said without hesitation that "your pharmaceutical company had the responsibility to inform me through my doctor that this drug was capable of producing 'adverse reactions' such as psychosis." The story reported that Nicholas and I were suing the company, the makers of the medication, to beef up their warnings and to highlight potential problems.

The Company Responds

During the next segment the reporter interviewed the medical director of the pharmaceutical company. He responded haughtily, calling the reporter by her first name, claiming extreme infrequency of serious side effects from the potentially addictive and powerful medication. It was reported that doctors and pharmacists also had the responsibility to inform patients about the "infrequent events." The medical director from the pharmaceutical company continued saying that changes in the label were just not necessary. The reporter asked him whose responsibility was it if the patient didn't get information about "infrequent events." The medical director for the pharmaceutical company said, "**I don't know.**" His segment ended there.

Our portion of the story concluded with my family conveying their conviction that it was the prescription drug that cost us young Nathaniel's life, and with final comments from my father and me. I expressed my deep gratitude for the gift of a child, as it was the greatest blessing we could ever have on this earth. My father, a grown man, wept while sharing from the depths of his heart his desire not to see another father have to tell his daughter that her little boy was dead!

Disappearing Act

After the interview aired I decided to contact Nicholas for moral support and so I searched for his phone number to give him a ring. I couldn't find it. I thought, *No worries I'll just call information and give them his name, city and state as I did after I read the newspaper article.* Information had no record of a Nicholas Jenkins. *How odd. I talked to him only a little while ago.* I called information three times, getting three different operators and still NO record of a Nicholas Jenkins. It was possible he had moved. I tried not to get overly concerned about it but it made me wonder.

I finally located Nicholas's phone number on a piece of paper in my filing cabinet. I called him. When he answered the phone I asked him if he had moved. He had not. I asked him if he had called the phone company to file for an unlisted phone number or have his number taken off their information list. He had not. I think I asked him the question two or more times because I was still in disbelief over the situation. How was it that it was so easy to get his number before through information, but now he seemed almost untraceable? He thought it was odd, too, and said he would check it out.

I called Peter to tell him the strange occurrence and he told me not to get overly excited about it. Then he went on to tell me the following story about a client that was paralyzed. The client's primary means of communicating and enjoyment was through contacting friends and family via the Internet as well as the attorneys with important information. When they began noticing the opposing attorneys filing depositions immediately following the client's correspondence regarding certain individuals, they realized they were gathering their information from somewhere.

Then correspondence went back and forth via email about a doctor who did not exist. When they received a deposition for the nonexistent doctor, they knew immediately the opposing side was casing their client through the Internet. It was Peter's way of saying don't be paranoid but be cautious. I wondered to myself what I was getting myself into. But my love for Nathaniel and his precious life overshadowed any fear I might entertain.

When someone questions the integrity of your character,
let it be that which strengthens you in Love and Truth
to forge ahead in the convictions of your heart.
—D.M. Roeder

My integrity was about to be challenged in a way that I had never dreamed was possible. Shortly after the airing of our story, a defamatory Website appeared about me on the Internet. It also attacked the host of the show along with everyone else who questioned drugging children. I had never met this person who claimed to know so much about me and my family. Seeing this Website made me angry at the insolence of the people or person perpetrating the Website, and only convinced me all the more that I was doing the right thing.

Jekyll & Heidi

It was also not long after the defamatory Website appeared that I encountered two of the most unusual characters I have ever met. Their names were Charles and Susan. They were the appointed attorneys who represented the defense for the pharmaceutical company. My first visit with them was when my attorneys and I flew to the southeastern part of the United States for me to give a mandatory deposition. We flew there because this was the region of the American headquarters for the foreign-owned company. My father came with me for moral support.

When Susan arrived in the deposition room to take her place across from us at the table, I remember thinking she was attractive. She was a slender woman with her hair pulled back in a tight bun. I felt at ease when I first saw her, grateful that a woman was on this case, thinking she would understand. She made it quickly apparent, by not making eye contact and by her callous questioning, that this was business and nothing was going to stand in the way of her success.

When Charles entered the room I had the opposite reaction. His appearance was not pleasing to the eyes. He had a pasty complexion with dark matted down hair, his nose came to a dull point and he had shifty eyes—shifty, that is except when he honed in to jam a dagger down your throat. I noticed that he was also thin and that he had rounded shoulders which gave the appearance that he was always hunched a little forward.

Charles's first words came when he looked at my father, who was waiting in the room with me, and said to him, "What the hell are you doing here? Get him the hell out of here!" I could see my dad's face turn fire engine red. It took everything he had not to haul off and plow Charles through his chair as he walked by him. I thought to myself, "You just disrespected my father."

Right after throwing my father out of the room, Charles put a piece of paper in front of my face and asked if it contained my handwriting on it. Still distracted from his disrespectful remarks toward my dad, I didn't ask to look closely at the paper and just confirmed yes. Peter, my attorney almost fell out of his chair. Peter and James later learned that my supposed handwriting was on a child support document where they alleged I initialed GED in the place of highest level of education. I was furious when I learned of this. I told Peter and James that there was NO WAY that I would ever have done something like this and that I was willing to take a lie detector test as well as have my handwriting compared to this supposed document by an expert. This was a blatant falsification. I felt the pharmaceutical company would use it to try and discredit my intentions for taking them to court. Peter and James felt downplaying it as a mistake would be a better way to handle it. I did not agree with this but I did not have much say because I leaned on their expertise—and reappear the form did during courtroom dramatics.

After my father left the room, I swore an oath that I would tell the truth and nothing but. After eight hours of deposition I could barely remember my name. I couldn't tell you everything we talked about in those eight hours, not because I won't but because most of it was a deluge of tidbits and fragments of medical data since my birth and every doctor I had seen and every medication I had "supposedly" been prescribed. But what I do remember most is that any time I would try to make reference back to the point of Nathaniel's death and the time surrounding it, Charles's eyes would set ablaze and he would yell, "That's not the question! Answer the question!"

During my deposition, James sat at the end of the table taking notes while Peter sat next to me. On occasion, I would try to glance at Peter when I felt that I was being swallowed up by the firing drill of questions. I could read encouragement and support from Peter's face. I noticed when he'd look at Charles he appeared to me as what a general might look like on the front lines as he led his troops into battle. He did not say a lot during the deposition, except during a few moments when he felt certain questions were out of line.

I noticed that Susan would slither back and forth in her chair, seeming to enjoy Charles's line of questioning. When it was her turn to ask questions, I thought for sure these two had come from the same womb. Her calculation was just as mean as Charles's. She seemed to take pleasure in harassing me with nonsensical questions without relevance and a universe away from the cause of Nathaniel's death. Here I thought this deposition was about the accident and the truth surrounding the event. I quickly came to learn it was about an execution. Mine.

When Charles and Susan decided they'd retrieved enough blood from my deposition, in closing, Charles pushed approximately thirty medical release forms in front of me to sign. Peter and James had warned me beforehand that I would have to sign them, so I did. When I was finished, Charles pushed about thirty more in front of me. I signed these too. Then he did it again and again. But I was prepared, because if my fingers fell off my right hand I had my left hand ready! I was not going away!

I went back to the hotel with my dad after the deposition was over. Exhausted, I went to my room, packed up my things and Dad and I got on a plane and headed back to Arizona.

Would'st thou both eat thy cake and have it?
—George Herbert

A week after my deposition at the pharmaceutical company's U.S. headquarters I got a phone call from some friends. They said a woman showed up in a brand-new, sleek, jet-black Lexus GS 400 with windows tinted black as onyx. They were a bit concerned because they said she cased their neighborhood for a couple days. Then she tried to make contact. It was Susan, without a subpoena. They refused to talk.

Soon after this I received another phone call. Louise, a good friend and former co-worker, called to tell me about a conversation she recently had. She said she spoke for close to forty-five minutes to a young woman about my employment, my character, my faith and everything else under the sun. Louise said she was grateful to help me in any way because she loved me and Nathaniel. I asked her who this person identified herself to be. She said the woman claimed she was working on my case against the pharmaceutical company.

Then, in a matter of a couple days I received a flurry of more phone calls. Jill, Marion, Rick and Sara were just a few who called to tell me about strange phone calls they received. Only this time a few of them had caught on in the middle of the conversation and asked the woman to identify who she was. It was at this point she told them she was Susan, who *represented* the pharmaceutical company. I immediately called Peter and James. They quickly made contact and sent her a letter regarding the issue of witness tampering. I highly doubt she stopped her antics.

Brenda was an eyewitness to my behavior on March 18. She, too, received an unidentified phone call prior to her deposition. On the day of her deposition, the pharmaceutical company fought not to have her deposition videotaped. They were on the phones with their high powered contacts. Brenda was stressed enough the day of her deposition. The pharmaceutical company made certain to drag the day out. They won. The deposition was not to be videotaped. Brenda did a valiant job at her deposition despite the enormous stress they put her under that day.

One day, Susan showed up unannounced at my worksite, questioning co-workers before I arrived. My supervisor asked her for a subpoena and when she couldn't produce one, threw her off the grounds.

The games and impositions these two played with the freedom that unlimited financial backing afforded them were without bounds. This backing placed the entire justice system at their disposal and they knew it.

Many well-intentioned people asked me a question I had often asked myself: "Why put yourself through so much pain and turmoil of a lawsuit that seems with every turn to stack the odds against you?" I'd cringe when they'd add, "You're young—you can have more children." Any parent who has lost a child knows how irreplaceable that child is, whether they have other children or not. Unfortunately, I did not have any other living children, but the love I experienced in having Nathaniel and raising him in that short amount of time reaped a harvest of love for a lifetime.

Depositions From Hell

It was not long after my deposition that a deluge of depositions were being called for by the pharmaceutical company. Individuals' lives were being inconvenienced and it bothered me very much, but I wasn't thinking much with my head these days. I was thinking more with my heart. The pharmaceutical company took depositions from friends, acquaintances, doctors, counselors, strangers and everyone they could find to drag out the process and pressure me to give up, which I determined not to do.

So when my attorneys called me to attend the deposition of a friend and told me I might hear the mention of my abortion I was shocked. I wondered to myself what an abortion fifteen years ago had to do with Nathaniel's death. Having already experienced the healing power of Christ in that painful situation, I realized this attack on my character struck at the very core of who I was and what I believed about God.

I believed that God's eternal nature was Love and Mercy. Because I had brought this very painful situation to Him in repentance in the Sacrament of Reconciliation many years before I experienced God's healing grace and restoration, I was forgiven.

To help me get through this deposition I reflected on the following words of Mercy from our Holy Father John Paul II. They are recorded in Evangelium Vitae and aided me in my healing journey after my abortion.

> *The Church is aware of the many factors which may have influenced your decision, and she does not doubt that in many cases it was a painful and even shattering decision. The wound in your heart may not yet have healed. Certainly what happened was and remains terribly wrong. But do not give in to discouragement and do not lose hope. Try rather to understand what happened and face it honestly. If you have not already done so, give yourselves over with humility and trust to repentance. The Father of mercies is ready to give you his forgiveness and his peace in the Sacrament of Reconciliation. You will come to understand that nothing is definitively lost and you will also be able to ask forgiveness from your child, who is now living in the Lord.*[4]

These incredible words of our Holy Father had helped mend the deep pain that the abortion had caused me. I saw the church in a new light. Not as one condemning and judging, but as one inviting me into its arms of compassion and mercy. The frequent reception of the Sacraments, along with the expert help of those trained to aid women and men in the recovery process after an abortion, was a shining blessing in my life. I was shocked that the pharmaceutical company would resort to such tactics to discredit my character, and that to mention my abortion was one of their most vile and merciless acts of hate against me.

An evil life is a kind of death.
—Ovid

What a wonderful time and blessing the young adult retreats had come to be in my life. I found an abundance of support there after my divorce and with the many social and prayerful opportunities provided to reconnect and continue to grow. I built life-long friendships that I still enjoy today. While out at restaurants, movies and outdoor events, many times bystanders would comment on the joy and laughter they saw us share amongst ourselves, and how refreshing it was for them to see a group have so much fun without the use of drugs or alcohol.

Since I anticipated that I'd enjoy life-long friendships with people I met at the retreat, when George showed up it wasn't a big deal to catch a bite to eat or have coffee with him. But as I shared earlier, his strange outbursts made me wary. And after he'd told me he had dabbled in devil worship, drugs and occult practices I got a sick feeling in my stomach. As a Christian I was called not to judge, but something told me I should end our acquaintance, which I did as politely as possible by making myself unavailable to return phone calls. With much effort on my part he finally left me alone.

Unfortunately, my having distanced myself from George came too late. Two weeks earlier I had acted on his recommendation of a doctor who treated ADD. George had commented that it was a coincidence that we both struggled with the disorder. It was at this time that I had decided to go back to graduate school to provide a better life for Nathaniel. I was looking for a doctor's direction and guidance regarding my attention deficit disorder. It seemed only reasonable for me to accept a referral from a person from our faith community.

The anger and bitterness I had at myself for taking a medication, even though I had no possibility of knowing what my reaction would be, was the most helpless of all feelings in the world. I was preoccupied with the if-onlys and the one that hung most heavily over my head was, "If only I had not taken this prescription medication." As Barbara D. Rosof states in *The Worst Loss: How Families Heal from the Death of A Child*:

> *A child's sudden death adds more tasks to the complex work of grieving. There is the brutal shock of learning the news. There are the emergency measures of denial and shock, and the searing pain as the shock response ebbs and the terrible reality comes home. With the reality comes the painful knowledge that there have been no good-byes.*[5]

I ached all over from the inside out, knowing that I would never be able to tell Nathaniel good-bye. Unfortunately, I hadn't any time for resolution of this missing piece or my anger toward myself due to George's constant home appearances and "helpfulness."

Two months after my release from the hospital still in shock and numb, George invited me to attend a hearing with him in downtown Phoenix. Since he'd "seemed" to be so helpful with my family and thinking it was for a traffic violation or something minor I agreed. He was vague about the purpose of the hearing. It was in the back of that courtroom I realized he had invited me to attend as a decoy of his deviant behavior. What I heard during this hearing horrified me. It turned out to be a trial for a custody battle between him and the grandparents of the little girl's mother, George's ex-girlfriend, who was in prison for drugs.

It was here I learned that the child was taken from George because, in a fit of rage he displayed against the little girl's mother, he took a handgun and began firing it in the house. In terror, the little girl hid under her bed. When the police came to the home, the frightened little girl would not come out from under her bed. After some time, she finally responded to the officers and was subsequently removed from the custody of George and the mother and placed with the grandparents.

Now I was hearing with my own ears confirmation of my earlier suspicions that George was an unstable person, and I remembered that this was why I ended our acquaintance prior to the accident. He told me he would kill anyone who got in the way of his getting his daughter. When he dropped me off at my house, I knew I needed to keep far away from him because my life and sanity depended on it.

Ending contact with George was not easy. He had conveniently made a "friend" with someone who lived across the street from my parents' house so he could be close to our home. He called constantly and showed up often unexpectedly. I was trying to work through the shock of my son's death and was not in a good place to deal with George's impositions. Having enough of his intrusiveness and violation of my privacy, I firmly told him that if he didn't leave me alone I would get a restraining order. Then George disappeared. I learned through a friend that he was spending time hanging around at a woman's shelter for pregnant moms. He eventually left town with one of these moms. I did not see him for five years.

It wasn't until after George "disappeared" that I learned about Nicholas and his tragedy. I shared with Peter and James my concerns about George. When the pharmaceutical company deposed George, Peter and James felt that for my safety it would be better that I not attend this deposition. They were always looking out for me and for this I was grateful.

Nathaniel's First Birthday

With fondness, I remember the excitement I felt during the time I prepared the celebration for Nathaniel's first birthday. The creative side in me wanted to make something special for him that shouted BOY to the world. What better way to do this than make a birthday cake in the shape of a race car. I found an amazing recipe in *Woman's World*, the weekly magazine. As I worked in the kitchen on the Daytona International Speedway creation, my Uncle John watched Nathaniel, who was taking to his new found hobby, walking. As I edged and smoothed, placed and tasted along the way, the shape of my son's first birthday cake came into being.

When it was time for family to gather for Nathaniel's birthday celebration, everyone oohed and aahed over the cake, which sat on the kitchen counter. It was nice to see their reactions, but with nervous delight I awaited the response of my number one fan.

After the arrival of the guests and after hugs and hellos were finished my dad placed Nathaniel in his high chair. My parents could hardly wait to lavish Nathaniel with gifts. When we finished opening a few gifts and ate our last morsels of dinner with eagerness, I walked over to the counter and picked up Nathaniel's cake. When I placed the cake in front of him he let out a little squeal. Then he smiled, kicking his legs back and forth in his high chair, and I was overjoyed to see that my son, at the tender age of one, appreciated the iced stock car before him. As Nathaniel dug into his cake and messed himself up with the frosting, I was mesmerized and thought I had witnessed one of the most amazing things I had ever seen!

Fourth Sorrow
Luke 23:27

"A large crowd of people followed Jesus"

I wonder about the sense of helplessness Mary might have felt upon hearing of Jesus's betrayal and judgment before the Sanhedrin. Did she experience fear and anxiety observing the tension and clamor of this terrible situation as it unfolded before her very eyes?

How is this possible, betrayed by one of His own? He could read your soul like He did the young woman at the well. Could my Son not have seen this coming?

He was found guilty before the chief priests and scribes. But how? Were these not the same men who'd heard Him speak in the temple at the age of twelve, being astounded by His answers? Where is their amazement now?

Was I not told by the angel at His conception that He would ascend the throne of David and He would rule forever with no end to His kingdom? Was I not told He would be great and be called Son of the Most High? Were not Joseph and I warned by an angel to flee to Egypt for the safety of His life? Where are the angels now? Where are the angels now?

The rise and fall of many, Prophet Simeon said, and the glory for the people Israel. Oh yes and Simeon mentioned the sword. Must it pass now? Sweet Lord, can we not have more time?

He was treated harshly, led like a lamb to the slaughter, and He opened not His mouth.[1] *Oh dear, my Son oppressed and condemned, Isaiah said, and taken away.*

But where?

I cannot bear to think of Your impending misery...but TRUST. I trust you my heavenly Father. I do not understand you but I trust in your will.

...and his mother kept all these things in her heart.[2]

Four

Pressing Through The Abyss

When I ponder what emotions Mary might have felt seeing her son Jesus carrying the cross on the way to his death, I wonder if a sense of helplessness and desperation visited her. I know for myself this is what I felt when my son's death was not being responded to in the way I had hoped by the FDA.

I had filled out the appropriate MedWatch form by way of the Internet. The form is the FDA's "Voluntary reporting of adverse events and product problems" contact. I received two "thank you" letters for reporting this event. *This is the death of a child,* I cried inside. I then called the FDA to speak to a representative, requesting help in answering some questions. I got shuffled around, and then I got a third letter thanking me for calling. I wondered if anyone from that organization was going to listen.

I contacted my local congressman and senators. I received a reply from one of my local congressmen. One. I still felt helpless because although the letter I received was more cordial than what I received from the FDA, it was not getting to the root of the problem, which was getting the word out about the potential deadly side effect of this drug. It was at this point that I contacted every congressman and senator in the United States, including email and hand-written letters to the president. I heard nothing for a very long time, so when I got a phone call from a collegiate magazine reporter who asked me if I was open to doing an interview for them regarding my tragedy, I took it to heart. I thought about the various news articles I had read on the abuse of the medication on college campuses across America, and how nobody seemed to be responding to the urgency of our tragedy. I agreed to do the interview. The reporter, Stephanie, took my information over the telephone. When I received a copy of the completed article in the mail I forwarded and discussed the article with close friends. They thought the reporter had done a great job.

When the courts tied up and prolonged our case year after year by folding to every stalemate procedure that the pharmaceutical company threw at them, I became frustrated. Nobody seemed to have the guts to push my case forward. I felt as if I had aged one thousand years. Then another attack came from a national attention deficit disorder Website. It posted an article that made false claims about me and the reporter of the collegiate magazine. The reporter of the ADD Website, whom I had never met or conversed with, made blatantly false accusations against me. I emailed the following letter directly to the reporter:

> *This email is in response to your Website and your accusation that I "blamed" the prescription medication for the psychosis that contributed to my son's death: and to the failure of Stephanie to mention the details of a police report—a police report that was taken under the immense duress and stress of a family and their friends trying to make sense of a tragedy that just occurred that day of March 18, 2000. The prescription medication caused my psychosis, period. I have never and I repeat never attempted suicide in my life. Am I without flaws? No. Without going into the details of my private life, as I'm certain the pharmaceutical company will manipulate/expose and misconstrue at their discretion, I unfortunately had a bad reaction to their medication. Am I here to say that it is a horrible drug and that it is incapable of helping anyone? No.*

But I am here to state that it harmed me and unfortunately led to my son's death.

The ADD Website not only failed to remove the journalist's article, but allowed the journalist to level more attacks against me. I contacted my attorneys. They sent a letter to the company that hosted the Website. It stated that the journalist's quotes alleging that the police accident reports said that I had a long history of psychosis, suicide attempts and psychiatric hospitalizations that began many years before I had ever taken the prescription medication were not accurate and that I had been hospitalized for treatment of depression while I was in graduate school. It said that I had never in my life attempted suicide before or since Nathaniel's death, and at no time up to the accident had I ever been psychotic.

Peter and James added that the ADD journalist's statement at the end of her story, noting that it was never okay for another journalist to break the law in pursuit of an article, should also say that it is never okay for a journalist to print that someone has had multiple suicide attempts and a long history of psychosis when such statements are just flat untrue. Peter and James requested on my behalf that the journalist and the ADD Website owners either produce documentation of the truthfulness of these statements or remove them from their Website. Peter and James assured them that a strong defamation case could be made by someone about whom inaccurate statements regarding mental illness have been made.

Within one month we were contacted by this ADD organization's counsel who telephoned, then sent in a letter to inform us that their client had removed all references about me from their Website. Peter and James recommended that I check the site on occasion to make certain they maintain their stance. Up to this time, the site has complied.

Deposition Of The Abuser

Just when I thought the company couldn't go any lower I learned otherwise. My attorneys called to inform me that they demanded to take the deposition of my childhood abuser. This deposition I chose to sit out. It was as if the pharmaceutical company bought and held an entire container of Morton's Salt and poured it over a wound that happened more than twenty-five years ago. The abuser's wife contacted my mom and asked her what the deposition was about. Then something amazing happened. My mother accepted her responsibility and broke the silence of denial. She told her sister the truth, how I tried telling her in my youth and how she dropped the ball by not doing anything about it back then. This irreverent intrusion on behalf of this company jump-started a new journey between my mother and myself as we confronted the pain of abuse head on, chose forgiveness and put that chapter of our lives to rest.

James told me that at his deposition the abuser denied all actions and accusations. Doesn't anybody believe in telling the truth anymore? Before the deposition I went into a fair amount of discretionary detail of the abuse with James, over the phone. He was my representing attorney at the abuser's deposition. My emotions ground with angst over the pharmaceutical company's incessant and arrogant invasions of my privacy, which convinced me all the more I was doing the right thing.

James later commented to me that if the abuser stated he had no knowledge of the assault, he admitted to a great amount of detail of a day he presumed to know nothing about. Under oath the abuser, like the pharmaceutical company, decided to deny responsibility.

I felt as if the abuser returned my forgiveness with a slap in the face.

The Pain Of Sexual Abuse

When I studied for my Master's degree in Counseling in 1993, one of my graduate course requirements was to participate in a small group in order to become acquainted with the dynamics of how small groups ran. Since I had already discussed my abuse issue with my counseling advisor, she suggested I attend a sexual abuse therapy group. I agreed, and thought this would be a good avenue for me to learn how to help young people who may have suffered from abuse, and perhaps I'd learn a little something helpful for myself, too. I had no idea what I was in for.

These small group sessions opened up the painful reality of the atrocity of abuse and its detrimental and damaging effects. I was no longer able to stand in denial over the affect it had had on me. As I attended the group with several ladies who had also experienced abuse, I began to recognize all the defense mechanisms which I had built as a barricade around my heart.

During this time I began to get overwhelmed, and fell into the pit of a depression. There were several factors attributing to my depression. This was the first time I was two thousand miles away from family and friends' support. In addition, being the driven person I am I strove for nothing less than straight A's which put a lot of pressure on me. Also during this time I was no longer taking the thyroid medication that had been prescribed for me at the undergraduate health clinic. I thought because my goiter had gone down, I wasn't supposed to take the medication any more.

Deep sadness seemed to overwhelm me, a pit I couldn't seem to lift myself out of. I was crying a lot. Bob and Sharon, friends who I had come to know, and who were also studying counseling, suggested that I get help. I agreed to let Bob and Sharon take me to the hospital. Nobody would see me there because I was not suicidal. The nurses told Bob and Sharon they would not permit my entrance to the facility unless I was suicidal. Begrudgingly, I fought for quite some time on this issue. Suicide wasn't an option because of my faith. Bob and Sharon in compassion said it was the only way I would be able to get the care I needed. Although I was not suicidal, I finally relented and signed the paper that stated otherwise in order to gain entrance into the facility.

What a terrifying experience this was. In the facility I was placed with souls struggling with obsessive compulsive disorder, anorexia, suicidal ideations and schizophrenia. I thought for sure I had gone to hell. Then, if this weren't bad enough in my weakened state, the nurses began to pump me up on all kinds of medications. I know they were only doing their job, but this begins what I call my 'Frankenstein' period. At this time I was put through a level of experimentation with drugging and dosing that made me become more depressed rather than better. I was released and back in the hospital three times over several months.

Yet as always there was a light that I found during this time and it resided in the suffering souls that became my "roommates." One gentleman who "roamed" the halls, and who some of the patients feared, one day came to share with me the trauma he had gone through when he opened the door of his teenage daughter's room to find that she had ended her life. He was not a monster but a wounded soul in search of help.

It was in this dark place I came to understand that in hardships and trauma there could be found a relentless pursuit to fight for life, and I realized that suffering and pain were a universal language.

When I left the facility I decided to take time off from school. I found an amazing job working as a lead teacher in the Head Start Program. My co-workers, students and their families brought me back to life, being the best medicine I had ever received.

He reminds me of the man who murdered both his parents,
and then, when sentence was about to be pronounced,
pleaded for mercy on the grounds he was an orphan.
—Abraham Lincoln

Peter said Charles was shaking when he entered the bathroom after he concluded the deposition with my father. Fumbling with his words, Charles fretfully asked, "Why, why, why did your client um… well um…well doesn't your client know that I only represent the pharmaceutical company?" To which Peter responded, "You are the pharmaceutical company to that family, and therefore you represent the death of their grandchild. The death of their daughter's child!"

Peter said my father had gotten an A plus during his deposition. Charles mistakenly asked my father the same question three times, trying to muddle reality. Charles asked my father whether I had ever left the house without Nathaniel in his car seat, to which my father responded, "No." After Charles's third attempt at building a house of cards in a hot wind, he asked my father again whether I had ever left the house, or had ever driven without Nathaniel in a car seat, to which this time Charles was met with my father rising out of his chair, leaning over the table and meeting Charles eye to eye saying, "Don't you understand English? No! My daughter has never left the house without Nathaniel in his car seat!" My dear dad stood firmly by me and by what he said on national television—that it was NOT his daughter who drove the car the day Nathaniel had died!

There is no other remedy for this evil of giving up prayer than to begin again...
—Teresa of Avila

My Uncle John was my dad's oldest brother, eight years his senior. Because three of my grandparents died when I was in grade school, my Uncle John became more like a grandparent to me. We were close, and he loved both my brother and me as if we were his own children. He was an uncomplicated man with a humor and wit that was as sharp as the crack of a whip. I laughed harder with him than with any other human being on the face of the earth. He never married. When I questioned him about this he said he was content and happy the way his life was, which could be seen in his genuinely jovial personality. But I wondered if the real reason might not have been because he had witnessed firsthand the long, agonizing months of the black lung disease that ravaged and robbed his father of his last breath. Black lung disease was what many of the coal miners in northeastern Pennsylvania got from working a lifetime in the mines. In addition, Uncle John shouldered solely of his own desire the responsibility of caring for his widowed mother until her own death many years later.

Uncle John had also fought in the Korean War, and when we talked about it, his face became somber as he remembered witnessing death firsthand. Although he could drive, he opted not to and he walked everywhere. He knew everyone in his town, and you couldn't go anywhere in Pittston, Pennsylvania without being stopped by people who wanted to chat with him or shake his hand. He was much, much loved and he was a neighborhood watchdog of sorts.

Uncle John had a broad build, like a tank, and hands that could crush a steel can in a wink. His heart was just as big, and everyone knew they could count on Uncle John for advice. The young would especially come to him because they knew he would tell it like it was, telling them many times what they didn't want to hear because he cared. Uncle John wasn't afraid to tell a teen father to do the right thing. The young man made a choice to have sex. Don't abandon the girlfriend and the baby, he would caution. To a girl dating a drunk, he'd say she was better than that, she was beautiful, don't let this man ruin your life. To a mom neglecting her child he'd say shape up, the kids need you, stop being selfish. To a dad physically abusing his children he'd say stop it, or I'll knock your block off.

He loved people with a great love, and I'd always said if he lived in another time and in another place he might have been a famous monk or something equal, because his love was larger than life. Yet he did not attend church. We, his family, often observed that a devotion to Jesus and Mary lived in him, as we could see in the completely worn-off face of Jesus that he had kissed so often on the crucifix that hung on the wall next to the front door of his home. Church and God lived bigger than life inside this man.

I loved him so much that I couldn't spend enough time with him, and when we moved away from him to Arizona I arranged every year for him to fly to Phoenix to visit us during Pennsylvania's roughest winter months. When he readied to leave for his visits with us he'd often tell his neighbors he was heading to paradise. We wanted him to move to Arizona, but his roots were deep in the people and the town he loved. We respected this and enjoyed immensely our time with him. We'd laugh so hard that we, too, experienced his paradise while in his presence.

There were countless times of enjoyment with Uncle John, but he was not left untouched by the devastation surrounding my decision to take this prescription medication. To his misfortune, he was visiting my family during the time I was prescribed and taking it. My drastic personality change caused me to viciously attack this person I loved so much. My parents and friends said in the few days before Nathaniel's death, I became paranoid and accusatory and verbally assaulted him telling him to stay away from Nathaniel. He said afterward he knew it was not me, but that he felt helpless as to what was happening. These days of tragic disturbance rocked and shook every one of us.

My sweet Uncle John returned to Pennsylvania, devastated by the death of his grandnephew, and did not visit with us again until the last years of his life. It felt as if the people I had loved with all my heart were gone in the snuff of a candle. As if this were not enough, my family and I came to discover that my uncle had had an unwelcome visitor in Pennsylvania years before, during the litigation period of my lawsuit. He shared with us how this visitor incessantly questioned him about my personality and my state of mind at the time that Nathaniel had died.

This upset my uncle very much. By the time my dear Uncle John came to live in Arizona during the last years of his life, he could barely see due to the diabetes that ravaged his body, and he had a failing kidney. I fear this unwelcome visit did not help heal his spirit but rather distressed him. He chose not to tell my family about it because he did not want to hurt me any more than I already had been hurt. I did not come to know about this until after the trial had ended. The thought that someone had questioned Uncle John and upset him made me furious. My attorneys confirmed that no deposition was held, and as to who the interrogator was we could only guess.

Fortunately, I had the opportunity to visit my uncle often during his days at the Paradise Valley Life Care Center. As he loved learning about the lives of people, I enjoyed reading him memoirs. One story he loved particularly well was *Forever Young*: *The authorized biography of the life of Loretta Young* by Joan Wester Anderson. We laughed, and I treasured his tale-telling as he reminisced about the old days.

My uncle lived out his last days as he had always lived, positively affecting everyone in the PV Life Care Center. The stories that the staff and volunteers shared with us about his loving humor and affectionate nature did not surprise us one bit. One such story told how he reached out to a young spastic woman who never came out of her room. He, being in a wheelchair himself encouraged her, through love and laughter, to get out of her room and into the halls and join in with the others. The nurses loved Uncle John, and this young woman's husband was grateful for my uncle's efforts. He commented on how a blind man seemed better able to see than those with clear vision.

After receiving the Last Rites of the Church, the reception of the Sacrament of Reconciliation and Holy Eucharist, the Good Lord took my Uncle John home on the Feast Day of His birth, Christmas Day, 2006.

Judge Lets Drug Maker Off The Hook

I trembled when I heard the news on that November day in 2002. How could this be? Nicholas's case had gotten thrown out of court in spite of the fact that drug-induced psychosis led to his child's death. The U.S. Magistrate, Judge Stephen Myers, dismissed the case, although the pharmaceutical company had previously admitted that their medication caused Nicholas to become completely psychotic, and that as a result of this psychosis he shot and killed his five-week-old daughter, Tara, and although the state dismissed all criminal charges against Nicholas, the Judge still held that the pharmaceutical company was not civilly liable.

The reasons given in the judge's opinion were that the label was adequate to alert the learned intermediary, which was the prescribing physician, about the danger of drug-induced psychoses. Even though the record before him demonstrated that the drug maker printed patient handouts with questions and answers about side effects, it had no duty to warn the actual users of their product about this side effect. FDA approval of the drug and its label preempted any state law claims relating to allegedly inadequate warnings. Sadly, this decision was likely a catalyst for doctors being joined as defendants in future cases.

Now it seemed there would be no recourse or accountability for Nicholas Jenkins's family on the part of this large pharmaceutical firm. It didn't seem fair. I hurt for Nicholas's family, who I'd gotten to know. They were the typical all-American, middle-class, hardworking family. They were devastated by the verdict. Nicholas's mom begged me to keep moving forward. I was shocked by the decision made in the courts. I thought, what chance did we *really* have, as it seemed we were fighting against a modern-day Goliath. I was shaken to my core.

Later on in that week I decided to go to the church to pray for an answer as to what I should do. Surely, I thought, I was going to get crushed by this company, which seemed to be able to slither out from responsibility using cruelty to their advantage, and the luxury of manifold precedents that filled the court system with red tape. Two children were dead and this wasn't enough to wake anybody up.

I prayed, I begged and I pleaded, "God where are you? Please give me an answer as to what I should do. Isn't it time to let someone else try and save the world from this situation? I don't know what to do. Please, please give me an answer to my prayer." I had brought with me a copy of *Magnificat Magazine* that I had not yet read. I sat, and feeling a little downhearted, I opened the magazine and randomly flipped to the following page:

What Sustained The Woman

Don't have any doubts about the divine assistance, don't turn in upon yourself because of the many calamities that continually surround you, for everything will turn out for God's glory and the salvation of your soul. Tell me, how can you doubt these assurances? Without divine grace, could you have come through all the crisis and battles which your soul has had to face in the past? So have confidence always, for all the rest will be done by this same grace: you will be saved and the enemy will be consumed by rage.

Continue to pray, meanwhile, and to give thanks and suffer according to the divine intentions and the divine will, and may you be encouraged to do this by the thought that your reward is not far off. I understand that the trial is hard, that the fight is unspeakably painful for your soul, but great is the merit of victory, ineffable the consolation, immortal the glory and eternal the reward.

You are afraid that your love for God is not true love, that you do not love God at all. Well, I urge you to be quite at peace on this point. Tell me yourself, do you not feel this love in your own heart? What is that ardent desire you feel in your soul? Who placed in your heart this yearning to love the Lord? Do you think that holy desires can be inspired by anyone but God?

Console yourself and be quite sure that God is not found where there is no desire for his love. Now, if the soul longs for nothing else than to love its God then don't worry and be quite sure that this soul possesses everything, that it possesses God himself.[1]

I looked at the bottom of the page to see who wrote these words that spoke directly to my soul and situation. I was stunned because they were written by my favorite saint, Padre Pio of Pietrelcina. Once again I was encouraged and strengthened for my journey. I shared the saint's words with friends.

An Email Of Encouragement

The stream of support from family and friends continued. Following is an example of an email of encouragement that I received from a friend.

Dawn:

Thank you for the inspirational message! I just had to print it out and place it on my bulletin board by my desk, where I can look up and see it daily.

Although you are still dealing with the legal aspects of the case and the trial, I also see you as a strong woman who has not let this tragedy rule her life. I see you as someone who is being a champion for a cause she knows is just, and a cause which is painful for her. But you are also someone who is living life. You are sharing with your friends, growing spiritually, supporting your family and friends, traveling, continuing your music ministry, being a great role model, etc. And I'm sure I don't know half of the things you are doing!

It really does not matter when the trial is. It would be nice to have it over, but it doesn't matter, because whenever they need you, you will be there. But in the meantime, live life, keep sharing and caring the way you do, and keep on growing and not letting anything stand in your way.

So...thank you for your strength and courage!

Sandy

Sandy is an amazing woman who herself has overcome obstacles with perseverance and faith. She is now a parent through a foster adoption program and a shining example of selfless love. Her words touched and helped embolden my spirit.

Not long after the judge let the pharmaceutical company off the hook in Nicholas's case, they attempted to get my case thrown out of the courts as well. This was only one of their innumerable attempts to do so. The following is an email I sent to the many people, both locally and across the nation, who were following the case:

> *At present, this past Tuesday a hearing took place, the pharmaceutical company filed another motion in the courts to have the case dismissed. As a friend and I were sharing,*

she asked me how hard it will then be if it is not dismissed and we go to trial, and in all honesty my response was that what would be even more difficult is never having an opportunity to go to trial in the first place. As you may understand we as a family have a strong desire to take the stand and simply share our story that it may be heard in a court of justice that the people may decide. But this may not come to pass and so I ask for your prayers for my acceptance of the outcome of this most recent hearing as God's Providence and Desire for what is best in our lives.

Also when my friend and I were sharing she mentioned one of my biggest struggles regarding saying yes to this suit in the first place, because no amount of money will ever bring Nathaniel back to me. She said what if the pharmaceutical company tries to make you out to look like a witch just after a fortune. That will hurt, but God knows my heart and what I have learned through this process is this case is SO much more than about money.

And yet perhaps the biggest thing has already been accomplished through these past many years is I have not backed down, but stood as that one small reminder in the back of their minds that there is another dead child who's mommy is not going away as they so often hoped and demonstrated through their merciless agenda. Thanks be to God and love for Mother Mary who has given me the strength to persevere.

The pharmaceutical company's most recent attempt to have the case thrown out of court had failed. We were moving forward. As part of the legal process, the company was permitted to have a psych evaluation done on me. I was not thrilled with the prospect, and I let my attorneys know this. "How fair was this really going to be?" I asked. Yet I knew it was a necessary evil and they could file grounds to dismiss the case if I said no. Once again I was on my way to the pharmaceutical company's U.S. headquarters on the east coast, but this time it was for a weekend of various tests and an evaluation with a forensic psychiatrist.

The first portion of my evaluation consisted of going through countless tests, including computer-generated ones, and written and physical strength tests. I spent most of the time with an assistant, a woman, who administered all the tests. Finally, after a day and a half of what I felt was their attempt to wear me down through testing, I had the joy of meeting their psychiatrist face to face. My attorneys fought to have my face to face evaluation videotaped, which it was. As I sat before the forensic psychiatrist, he assigned another doctor to sit behind me. Parallel to me was the young lady who sat and tape recorded the session. I didn't spend very much time with the psychiatrist. He asked me a few questions regarding the sexual abuse and then drilled me on one specific area regarding my memories of the accident. When he'd gotten what he'd wanted he looked with a quick smirk at the doctor behind me and said that will be all. I didn't see him again after that. I would estimate that my total amount of time with him was little more than an hour. I came to learn later that the doctor who was sitting behind me wrote and submitted his report on Nicholas before ever having seen him!

I wrote an email to my attorney, Peter:

Peter,

You know what? I am sooo wanting this lawsuit to be over so that I can start living my life. I feel like I've been in bondage to this thing forever. Yeah, I know, like everyone I talk to says, hang in there, you're so close, but I will be honest with you—it has taken an exorbitant amount of energy to keep my heart and head in this thing and I'm not sure it's really been worth it. Thankfully, my parents didn't disown me after my venting on them.

Sure my desire has been from the beginning to help people and to make sure that Nathaniel didn't die in vain. But what the heck does that mean anyway!? Who on earth ever dies in vain? Remind me why I'm doing this, please! Really, is this really going to help anyone? It's truly difficult when you don't see any direct positive results...and, if anything, what good is going to come of Charles and Susan humiliating me and my family on a witness stand any more than they already have, as their drug has already robbed me of Nathaniel and my peace of mind?

Thank you for letting me be frank and honest. I know you've busted your butts on this thing and so have I. I'm not bowing out unless I get a direct sign from the big Guy upstairs. Maybe He's already given it but I've been too stubborn to listen. Good God, forgive me if this is so.

I was exhausted and worn out, but deep in my heart I wanted to persevere.

Peter's response:

Dawn Marie...it is certainly natural for you to have reservations about your case...most of our clients do. Our civil justice system is a behavior modification system. They don't put gas tanks in the impact area on cars, don't make flammable children's pajamas, don't sell Dalkon Shields and don't have asbestos in classrooms now...all because of lawsuits. We like to think that every case we file makes a difference in some way to somebody. Your's included. Keep the faith amiga...Peter

Courage consists, not in blindly overlooking danger, but in seeing and conquering it.
—Jean Paul Richter

Two-thirds of the way through the process of the case I was called to attend a mandatory mediation that was set by the courts. I flew back east once again. I met with James and Jason Collins. Jason was one of the youngest attorneys on our team. He represented local counsel for my case. While on our way to the mediation, James mentioned to Jason that Kim, the woman who was chosen to mediate our session, was an acquaintance of Charles. It was at this moment I realized that I flew a long way for lunch.

If you have ever seen the movie *Rainmaker*, you will get a good visualization of what I walked into when I entered the mediation room with James and Jason. There were two representatives from the pharmaceutical company as well as Charles and Susan. Composing myself, I humbly embraced my herald, "Keep On Charging The Enemy So Long As There Is Life" in my heart, and held a relic in my hand, given to me by a friend, and sat down. It was gut wrenchingly difficult facing the individuals who I felt contributed to the end of my son's life. I reflected upon some comments made by well-meaning individuals. They shared with me how they understood why the case was so difficult, because I was up against a soulless institution. I can tell you this, when I walked into that room it wasn't a ghost that I saw sitting in front of me, but individuals with the power to decide for right and wrong.

The initial part of the mediation was a time where both sides of the lawsuit, which were now face to face, made formal statements. I decided prior to the meeting that even though I had A LOT to say, it was better for me at this time to defer all comments to my representation. Our face-to-face statements were made. I searched from each person present for some semblance of compassion, but once again found none and noticed that during opening comments Susan failed to look me in the eyes the entire time. Then a brief discussion ensued with Charles making most of the comments.

Charles made the huge mistake of saying that because I had psychosis prior to taking the prescription medication, this case was not even going to make it to trial. He might as well have said to me that your son wasn't worth crap and all the effort you are going through for him was a waste of time. That was what his arrogant remark said to me.

Not long after Charles's insolent comment, both teams went into separate rooms for discussion. Kim stated that once we were in separate rooms, whatever we shared was open for discussion with the other side unless otherwise specified. What happened next raised the hair so high off the back of my neck it was a good thing we were in separate rooms, because I probably would have jumped across the mediation table and done something I would have regretted.

Kim entered dialogue with James about how it wouldn't be such a bad thing if your client had had psychosis prior to the prescription medication incident. This was an obvious loophole I felt the company was trying to force to negate their responsibility. It was at this point I could remain quiet no longer. I had had enough of the pharmaceutical company and their attacks on my family and on my personal character; enough of their attacks on my motherhood, my integrity as a woman and attacks on my faith. I reflected on their sixty plus depositions. James commented he had not seen this many taken by a company in the long history of his representation. I remembered their invasion of every shred of privacy I might have ever had. Exasperated I remembered how Charles was disrespectful to my father and how he now, once again, disregarded and was disrespectful to my son.

While I didn't slam my fist on the table I planted them firmly, looking Kim straight in the eyes. I told her that I had had enough of the bull____ and that she could tell the pharmaceutical company representatives that I would see them in court!!! That ended mediation. I flew home that day.

The loneliness I felt during the litigation process sometimes felt overwhelming. I had never been involved in a lawsuit before nor did I have any friends or family who had been involved in one. I felt as if I were in unchartered territory without anybody to talk to. I had confidence in my attorneys' ability to convey the truth, but as time and the odds stacked against us, I felt discouraged. Still, I was unwilling to give into it for very long because of my love for Nathaniel, and I believed that although things appeared as though they were hopeless, it was not because my faith lay not in the government, or in any one person or thing, but in the God who is beyond understanding. And just when I would think I could go no further, He'd send me a sign.

It happened after friends sent me email that MTV was hosting a program they thought I should watch. The program was about the medication and the harm it was causing a few college students. I felt sad and weary that nothing significant seemed to be getting done to protect these individuals, so I drove myself to Our Lady of Perpetual Help church and went into the adoration chapel to pray. As I sat in silence before the majesty of Our Lord in His Blessed Sacrament, a song rose up in my heart and I began to sing what words I knew of it.

After a moment, I realized I was stuck and that I didn't know the entire song, but only the refrain. I looked in the pew and shuffled through several music books to search for the song but couldn't find it. So I held the title of the song in my heart and continued my prayer.

Then Sunday came and I went to church, as it was time for me to prepare with the rest of the choir to sing for mass. When the music director handed out the songs to be sung I was astounded. There before my eyes on the song sheet was the very song I was trying to remember. I think I freaked the director out a little bit because I jumped up and said I can't believe this. I began to share with him what had happened to me that prior week. He said it must be something special because the entire year he had only chosen this song one other time.

Below are the words of the refrain. They remind us, no matter the outcome of the challenges set before us, we are His children and He has amazing and blessed plans for each one of us:

Do Not Fear To Hope

Do not fear to hope though the wicked rage and rise.
Our God sees not as we see, success is not the prize.
Do not fear to hope for though the night be long.
The race shall not be to the swift, the fight not to the strong.

—Rory Cooney

I wrote another email to Peter.

Peter!

In laymen's terms please. Has the Motion to Dismiss the case BEEN DISMISSED? Does this mean we are moving forward? I know there is still a road ahead of us, but this means we're moving forward doesn't it?!!!

Dawn Marie

You would be right, Dawn Marie...Motion to Dismiss was DISMISSED and we **are** *going forward.*

Congratulations, amiga...Peter

A month before trial, George mysteriously reappeared after five years. He began to show up at the same events that I attended. One day my mom picked up a strange phone call from someone called Steven. Instinctively knowing something was wrong, she began rigorously questioning him. He claimed he was George's cousin. She told him not to call again.

A week before the trial my attorneys informed me of a new development. The attending judge on the case had been replaced. James and Peter were told the new judge would be fair for us. *Hmm*, I wondered to myself, *I hope they are right and I am not walking into a lion's den*. It was not long after this that I told Peter in a phone conversation the thing I was most afraid of, and that was, if we lose this case, would I feel as if I had lost Nathaniel all over again?

Arizona Cardinal's "Pick Your Seat Day"

One of my fondest memories with Nathaniel was the day that his Papa and I took him to the Arizona Cardinals "Pick Your Seat Day" in May of 1999. This was the day when Arizona Cardinals fans could see the football team practice at the stadium, and afterward were permitted to go down onto the field and meet the players and coaches. Nathaniel was in rare form that day and his excitement was so dear.

I remember the joy he expressed as he listened to the music playing over the loudspeakers as he hummed and bobbed in my arms. Then he leaned over to grab the hat off the little boy standing next to us. When Papa decided to place Nathaniel on his shoulders, Nate was so elated by the experience it was as if he were given all the ice cream he could eat in the world.

I will never forget the energy and enthusiasm Nathaniel displayed over his surroundings when it was time to go down onto the field. He practically burst out of my arms and ran onto the football field. A chase ensued as I kept a watchful eye over his endeavors. He could not run fast enough or greet and hug enough of the children whose paths we crossed.

Then he did something so sweet and curious it caught me off guard. He began to run with a full burst of energy, then he would dramatically stop, bend and drop his little torso and look between his legs. I knew this was something important to him because he began to do it often and from every angle of the field, enjoying the world from his new "perspective." I smiled at Nathaniel's enthusiasm, at the wonder of a child finding such joy and pleasure in the simple things of life.

Fifth Sorrow
John 19:25

"Standing by the cross of Jesus were his mother"

I wonder about the pain and sorrow Mother Mary must have felt in seeing Jesus hanging nailed to the cross. Was this not the child She bore and nursed and loved, keeping careful watch over His every step and growth into maturity? Sure He was God, but He was no less Her Child.

"Away with this man." *Their shouting, I cannot bear to hear it.* "Barabbas!" *They call for the release of this man, but he is a murderer and my son a healer...**a sword**.*

Pilate wishes to release him, my son, oh please do. Their shouting is unbearable. "Crucify him! Crucify him!"[1] *What will Pilate do? They spit on him, scourge and kneel before him, they mock him...Oh dear, their shouting, it has prevailed...**a sword will pierce**.*

Where are they taking my son? The Skull! Golgotha.[2] Take your son, your only son whom you love.[3] *Heavenly Father, is this not the place... only a short distance...the same mountain on which Abraham laid the wood to offer up Isaac?*[4] *You gave him back his son good Father, please...**a sword will pierce your own heart.***

...condemned, between two criminals, three hours long...

...the stripping, the crown, the mockery, the nails, the Cross... He speaks. "My God, My God." *Oh God, not forsaken!* "It is finished." ***A sword will pierce your own heart, too.***

...he was pierced for our offenses[5]

...one soldier thrust his lance into his side, and immediately blood and water flowed.[6]

I no longer fear suffering, for it has arrived. There is no escape, it is here. But…I TRUST. I trust you my heavenly Father…I do not understand you but I trust in your will.

…and his mother kept all these things in her heart.[7]

FIVE

WHAT IS TRUTH?

—PONTIUS PILATE

SINCE 1981, IN THE FORMER Yugoslavia in a village called Medjugorje, located in Bosnia-Hercegovina, the Blessed Virgin Mary had been reportedly appearing to six people—Ivan, Jakov, Marija, Mirjana, Vicka and Invanka—and through them she has given messages for the world. She told the visionaries, *"I have come to tell the world that God exists. He is the fullness of life, and to enjoy this fullness and peace, you must return to God"*.[1]

My first trip to Medjugorje was for the Feast Day of Mary's Assumption, August 15, 1988 and how I came to learn about Medjugorje was by way of a unique set of circumstances. My priority when I arrived in Arizona in January 1986, was to find work and establish my one year residency so that I could attend Arizona State University (ASU) for my Bachelors Degree in Elementary Education. Because I was not able to afford out-of-state tuition, I found a job working as a waitress for the Left Seat Restaurant at the Scottsdale Airport. It was enjoyable work and I met many wonderful people.

As my one-year anniversary approached, I planned to leave this north Scottsdale location and move south to the city of Tempe so I could be closer to ASU. It was at this same time my younger brother moved to Arizona after graduating from high school in Pennsylvania. He was looking for employment and so I referred him to the owners of the Left Seat Restaurant. They hired him and he began working there shortly after my last day. During Tony's employment he met and made friends with an elderly couple who dined at the restaurant and had come to love him. Tony grew quite fond of them, too. They enjoyed sharing their Catholic faith with him and in the course of their conversations, they began to tell Tony stories about a far-away land where there had been reported events of a supernatural nature. The land they talked to my brother about was called Medjugorje, a place in which innumerable peoples of diverse cultures sojourned there from all parts of the globe.

My brother would come home from work and tell me stories about this land of visionaries who reported seeing apparitions of the Blessed Virgin Mary, whom they'd come to call Our Lady Queen of Peace. "Who is this Lady?" I inquired, never having heard of Fatima or Lourdes. Medjugorje sparked my interest and when my brother was given a book by this couple called *The Queen of Peace Visits Medjugorje*, by Father Joseph A. Pelletier, I read it enthusiastically before the book ever hit the coffee table.

Before I knew it my brother was in a plane on his way to Medjugorje, a gift from this elderly couple, and within me grew the longing to go, too. But as school was starting, money was tight. I said a prayer that would be answered one year later: "Dear Mother, I believe if it is God's desire for me to go to Medjugorje, you will provide a way," and she did. I attended a prayer service at St. Maria Goretti Church, where I met this same couple for the first time. Someone had shown a picture they brought back from Medjugorje, and after watching me standing in awe of it, the elderly gentleman said to me, "You pay for your Visa and we'll pay for your trip." I think my jaw must have dropped and hit the floor because I fumbled around with words not being able to speak, and he said in a sweet yet direct way, "You heard me, you pay for your Visa and we'll pay for your trip." This elderly couple, too old to travel there themselves, had extended this most incredible gift to my brother and now to me.

I could speak for hours of the miracles I witnessed while there: the dancing sun you could look directly into without hurting your eyes; the cement cross on Mount Krizevac in midday, beaming a brilliant light which could be seen from miles away; or this same cross in a cloudless sky, disappearing completely from view and then reappearing; a multitude of bright stars filling the sky during the day; and on and on. But I would come to learn the most precious thing coming out of this land was the prominent message, not of all the outward signs, but of the inward sign of conversion—conversion of heart through prayer, a turning away from sin and death and a turning toward Our Loving Creator with all of our hearts. Peace comes through this and without the action of prayer it is impossible.

Yet with these extraordinary happenings in this land since 1981, although Medjugorje itself was left untouched, Mostar, parts of Bosnia and outlying regions were struck by war and devastation in 1993.

I was fortunate to have the opportunity to go to the blessed land of Medjugorje again during my lawsuit. Knowing it was going to be some time before we actually went to trial, my attorneys told me to go, rest and enjoy my time. I went there because I needed strength and I found it there.

I will never forget a special moment I experienced as I climbed the ominous 1,750-foot rock and thorn bush covered mountain, on which at its top, was affixed a 33-foot-high cement cross. This huge mountain received its name for that votive cross. It's called Mount Krizevac, which stands for Cross Mountain.

The cross was built in 1933 as a vow Father Bernardin Smoljan made in hopes of uniting his famine and poverty stricken parishioners to commemorate the 1900 years since Christ's death. His parishioners agreed, and some of them barefoot in an act of sacrifice carried heavy bags of cement, iron bars, wooden beams and other necessities to the top. "Holy Relics—parts of the Crucifix of Christ, brought especially from Rome, were placed at the intersection of the

Cross." Upon its completion Father Smoljan dedicated his parish to Christ, the Saviour of the world to protect it from any evil.[2]

Today on Mount Krizevac there are beautiful bronze carved representations of Jesus Way of the Cross which align a path to the top. As I made my way up the mountain with a group of forty pilgrims from every part of the world, I received inspiration when we stopped to pray at the Sixth Station of the Cross. This station represents the longstanding Catholic tradition of the story of a woman named Veronica. In a moment of impassioned charity, Veronica leapt from the crowd toward Our Lord as he carried His cross to Mount Calvary to die. In a brave feat, not minding the soldiers in the way, she fell to her knees in front of Jesus, stretched forth her arms and hands in solace, and wiped the blood and sweat from His face with her veil. Her heroic effort afforded her the mighty gift of the impression of our Lord's face upon her veil. On the Via Dolorosa in Jerusalem there is a small chapel known as the Chapel of the Holy Face. Traditionally, this is regarded as the home of St. Veronica and site of the miracle. There, in her very name, lies great mystery: "Vera," meaning "true," and "icon," meaning "image." Words flowed through my heart: *Thank you for giving your life for the children.* I was struck by an overwhelming peace and joy.

The Friday evening before we flew east for the lawsuit, Peter and I chatted a bit. He followed up our phone conversation with an email which was exactly what I needed to hear to ready myself for battle.

> *Dawn Marie...you need to know this, and you need to know this right away. James and I believe in you and believe in your case. We didn't have to represent you. We pick our cases very, very carefully. You're our friend. We love you. What happened to you on that March morning never should have happened. We can't change that.*

You had a choice to either ignore the fact that people weren't being told about the dangers of this drug or to do something about it. You chose the latter. It's been terribly hard for you to fight through all the corporate/Charles bullshit...but you've done it. You've already made thousands and thousands of people aware. Now, it's almost over. The jury wants to hear from you. You'll do just fine, Dawn. The Holy Spirit will be hovering over the witness stand while you're on it. Nate will be watching. You'll be at peace. What a great opportunity, right?

See ya over there...Peter

Before the trial, I wrote the following email to the dear people who were following my lawsuit.

Hi Friends and Family,

I will not be communicating via the Internet until the trial is over. You may get updates of the trial at www.(my attorneys Website).com.

On behalf of Nathaniel, my family and myself, from the bottom of our hearts we are sincerely grateful for your prayers and support.

Love you and God bless you,

Dawn Marie

www.Nathaniellives.com

The idea to create a Website for Nathaniel developed as a passion in my heart coming from a deep need I had to express my love for my son and to honor his beautiful life. I developed the site shortly after Nathaniel's death with the help of a Webmaster I chose out of the Yellow Pages. It was full of pictures of Nathaniel and commentary by family members and friends who knew Nathaniel. In it was included a homepage with dozens of pictures of him with his grandparents, his dad, me and the many people who loved him dearly. Included on the homepage was the prayer that was handed out at his funeral mass.

The second page included a memorial page and a beautiful picture of my son with a letter I'd written, now that he was in heaven. Included in the memorial section were Cardinal's Day camp pictures, grandparent pictures, and friends and birthday pictures. This section ended with a beautiful song that my brother wrote to Nathaniel, entitled "We Will Meet Again."

The second section of the site was titled "What Happened?" It included the topics: "I never thought it could happen to me," "My history with ADD," "Frustration and developing my own techniques," "Successes," "Events of the Tragic Day," and "My Farewell."

The third section of the site was titled "Acknowledgements and Support." It included: "Messages of Support," which displayed hundreds of thank you notes to people whose loving prayers and support we could not have made it without, plus "Faith and Testimony," "Support Groups and Contacts," and a "Helpful Books" section of fifteen books I had found helpful in dealing with sudden death syndrome. This section also included links to specific organizations, such as Compassionate Friends and M.I.S.S. Foundation, that dealt with the death of a child to aid persons in the grieving process.

Later I added an "Update" section on the progress of the lawsuit, or lack thereof, and an "In the News" section that listed newspaper links and articles that friends across the nation had emailed to me regarding the challenges the prescription medication was facing all over the country.

The pharmaceutical company made a motion to try to get the Court to order us to take *www.Nathaniellives.com* off the Internet during the trial, and to try to get James and Peter to take everything about the medication off their attorney Website. James responded to the judge that we would be glad to agree, IF it applied to both sides—that is, if they took their medication Website off the Internet and eliminated everything about their medication from their company Website during the trial.

As you might imagine, their motion fell into the mud.

My Journal Entries

January 7th, 2006

12:45 p.m.

We've departed and we're bound for the pharmaceutical company headquarters. People keep saying good luck and it strikes me very odd. Good luck, like it's a game of craps or something—I don't think so. There is something much more at stake here than a bucket of cash. Lives, dignity, honor and integrity. They, the pharmaceutical company say you're scum, I say I'm not. They say you're dirt, I say I'm blessed, they say we're going to kick your butt and I say here's the other cheek,—a little sarcasm. I think of Father Joe's analogy several months ago of what giving the other cheek to your enemy really means. He said, "Walk with your head held up not looking down in defeat, not in defiance or arrogance but in dignity that your words may sting and your slander might knock me down a little but in love both for you and for myself I hold my head up and pass you to say in peace that no offense is taken or on the way."

1:30 p.m.

At reconciliation last night at St. Jerome's I met with a priest I never saw before. He looked like he might be from India. I went face to face. I shared my pain and angst over leaving for trial the next day. This is not who I am. I am not an angry person but it has unfortunately come down to a case of name calling as they choose to sling mud and string things out in the system. The priest did not speak for some time and I began to wonder if he understood anything I said. I shared some more saying how difficult it was for me and what a struggle to forgive my enemies...And then Father began to speak and he said that "just anger" is good, that there is a time for anger and that there is a time for forgiveness. Even Jesus expressed anger...Thank you Father for giving me permission. I'm not ready to forgive the pharmaceutical company yet.

2:04 p.m.

I'm going to listen to uplifting music right before I take the witness stand—some time that day. Blessed Mother will be with me, she knows what it is like to lose a son.

2:20 p.m.

"...And I'm proud to be an American cause at least I know I'm free"

God bless the USA[3]

5:30 p.m.

East Coast time

We're about to land. Touch down soon... I'm here. I've arrived on enemy territory—home turf and the headquarters of foreign owned pharmaceuticals...could you please tell me why it is you don't sell your drug in your own country!

God bless the USA

What lies ahead?

9:30 p.m.

Met with Peter, Joe and Catherine. Joe was the young man who set up technical equipment to be used during trial. Catherine was an attorney who worked for Peter and James's firm. Joe and Catherine traveled nineteen hours from San Antonio...must be exhausted. Dear Lord please let this be a time of healing and strengthening for my family, please grant my folks a peace filled sleep, heal our memories, mind and emotions. Mom has become a little nauseous. We're all stressed. Lord bless the outcome but most of all the journey, bless the journey...my heart is broken for some time. I truly hope for some healing of heart and peace of mind.

My parents well being is a concern for me. Is this going to be too stressful for them? I checked with them often through the years. I gave them progress reports and asked for their feedback.

I told them that I did not need to do this. I knew my son was in heaven. Right up until the very last week I checked with them and their answers were always the same. We support whatever decision you make Dawn. This is your call, we will support you either way.

January 8, 2006

6:40 a.m.

Rough's night sleep. Not wanting my dirty laundry to become public domain. Lord you were pure, you were innocent and free from sin. Lord most of your saints were too. I'm a sinner...

2:40 p.m. Sunday

Mass was absolutely beautiful. Mary Queen of Heaven Church, my precious Nathaniel is buried at Mary Queen of Heaven Cemetery.

I want to cry. I want to scream right now, so many things I want to say, so many things I want to do, finish reading Charlotte's Web with Nathaniel. I want him here. I want to hold him. He was definitely present in spirit at Mass. What a special priest. What a special service. Everyone in this small church sang and participated. Today is the Feast of the Epiphany. The priest talked about the importance of boundaries. How we have to respect and keep each other accountable by boundaries and what a good thing this is—so true—in marriage what's acceptable or not—with our children for safety and growth in respect—and I think to myself clear boundaries between the FDA and the pharmaceutical company.

The Responsorial Psalm was:

"The justice of the Lord shall flourish and the fullness of peace forever."

What are you going to bring up to assault me Charles... what stones are you going to throw?

5:50 p.m.

Just got a phone call from Peter. He said we're to meet in the 'war room' at 6:00 that's 10 minutes from now to go over some strategic stuff to get acclimated for tomorrow, when's and what to expect kinds of stuff...

11:15 p.m.

It's the eve of trial or as some have said, "my day in court."

After jury selection Dad is supposed to go first. Go grandpa. Then James's introduction and several taped depositions of vital information. I hope it's permitted. That's when the war begins... will the media be there, will it be calm, will they attempt settlement...not without a label change—will they forgo settlement... gear for battle...

January 9, 2006

6:30 a.m.

The morning of the trial.

I'M STILL HERE!

Was I frightened when I entered the courtroom to take my seat in the jury stand to be present during jury selection? Oh you bet. I was terrified. I trembled. I never knew that human cells could shake, but I am certain this was the case because from my toes to my head I trembled on the inside. Why? Because I felt completely powerless. My life was now in the hands of others, my case to be fought over by others, and the verdict to be judged and given by others.

I was not naive. I had been witness to the hideousness and heartlessness of the opposing attorneys during the endless depositions I attended, and their constant badgering of potential witness testimony for our side. My friend Rick said that Susan called him so much he had finally gotten so upset that he yelled at her, telling her he knew my character well, thought I was an amazing person and that she was not going to get anything out of him to the contrary. He told her to stop calling him.

Charles's cordiality gleamed brightly too during the litigation process. He had previously disrespected my father, telling him to get the hell out of the deposition room; he disrespected Nathaniel when he said this case wasn't going to make it to trial; and he yelled at me when I mentioned Nathaniel's name during my deposition.

He made it clear this case was not going to be about a child. There would be no personalization in this case. It was solely about the destruction of my character without a quest for truth whatsoever. In fact there was never, at any point during the entire litigation process, any demonstration from this company of a search for genuine justice. They had made it evident from the beginning that it was about search, seize and destroy. I was fully ready to accept the circumstances, not wanting to blame, but get to the bottom of why I reacted so horribly to their medication.

So was I shaken when I entered the courtroom, because of the terrorism I had experienced by this opposing company and the lack of a constructive response from the FDA? Oh sure I was. But I was not going to let it show, not one iota of fear would you see from me. Oh dear God, the energy it took to remain composed, a torrential amount, but I didn't move. I didn't quiver. I didn't shake. I was there for my son and no devil in hell was going to take that away from me!

More journal entries.

8:14 p.m.

Jury selection took about all day—and then came James and Charles's introductions. James's opening statement was a solid point... that this pharmaceutical company warned by sending a letter to all their distributors and doctors when their chemical plant burned that this would pose no obstacles to supply and demand but when the VP admitted Nicholas's case of psychosis and the death of his child, no warning letter was sent to distributors or doctors regarding this. Then Charles's presentation: Oh my God... what the hell does stockpiler mean? Charles missed his calling. He should be making science fiction movies. His powerpoint presentation was abominable. What did I ever do to him to deserve such hatred and such lies. James was right when he said after mediation..."YOU HAVE NO CONSCIENCE." I'm going to get killed in this case... no matter...I don't have to win or lose...I'm doing it for Nathaniel... I'm doing it for others... somebody has got to hold this company accountable... it certainly doesn't looks like the FDA is going to!

...that was so hard and now to see my family worry about me, again.

January 10, 2006

Today was a better day than yesterday. Today Dad took the witness stand and he did a great job. It was difficult to see him do this. He showed strength and love for his grandson and shared how proud he was of me. He spoke of my intelligence and my work in ministry and volunteer work abroad. They attacked him and he held strong. Mom goes tomorrow...

Very comforting phone calls...many, many are praying for us.

The next two days were a blur of information and insults. I rested whenever possible and did not journal until the day I took the stand.

An article I read in *The New England Journal of Medicine* stated,

> The loss of a child is one of the most severe forms of stress, on a par with the death of a parent in childhood. A large survey based on Danish records shows that for some, it can lead to psychiatric hospitalization...The death of a child under age eighteen raised the risk of

> psychiatric hospitalization by 78% in mothers and 38% in fathers. For depression, the most common cause of hospitalization, the excess was 91% for women and 61% for men... Loss of an only child raised the risk most...[4]

Post-traumatic Stress Disorder

A year and a half into the grieving process, the shock and numbness began to wear off and searing pain began to set in. It was also during the time of the upcoming holidays, which for many who've suffered loss brings the aching void to the surface. I had no plan to end my life but I was so depressed that I asked for help. Due to insurance reasons I requested to go to a specific facility which had an extensive day program in Tucson. When I got there, I was once again immediately pumped up with medication with names I'd never heard of before, and once again instead of getting better I got worse.

By God's grace I was then relocated to another medical facility where I met a woman named Lisa, who worked for a renowned trauma center. Her response after meeting with me for several sessions was, "What in the heck were you doing at that facility. It's a drug and alcohol rehab. You're not crazy nor are you suffering from drug and alcohol addiction. You have post-traumatic stress disorder. You have a road ahead of you. You can do it, but you have a road ahead of you."

I was disheartened by her comment of the road ahead but grateful for her honesty. Now I was able to put a name to all the pain and confusing emotions I was going through. The medical facility immediately took me off all the medications that I had been placed on at the previous facility, and I began working intensely with Lisa. I began getting better and stronger every day.

Dawn...got your voicemail. Did Cathy's depo hurt us? [Cathy was a nurse at Facility X] Well, yes and no. The Facility X records are the only place that psychosis is mentioned. She said that if she'd seen psychotic behavior she would have written it down. She didn't. So, if they're going to use the records to prove you're psychotic, why didn't they depose the doc who said he saw it. Also, his paragraph about no hallucinations or delusions really, really waters it down. Bottom line is that I wish it wasn't in the record, but it is, and we have to deal with it, and it's a very controllable, explainable observation. On the other hand, Cathy really stung them with her other patient who'd gotten psychotic on amphetamines. Are they going to argue that Cathy's not qualified to testify about that because she's not a doctor? Possibly. But if they do, then they can't get anything into evidence about the psychosis they asked her about. The depo was at the very least a tie for us. Don't worry, my friend...we're okay...Peter

The doctor was never deposed.

Eye Movement Desensitizing And Reprocessing—EMDR

I met Sophie shortly after my work with Lisa. Sophie was a Master's in Counseling professional with many years of specialization in the treatment of post-traumatic stress disorder and the Eye Movement Desensitizing and Reprocessing (EMDR) technique. I learned about EMDR through Jennifer, my mom's best friend. Jennifer shared with us how helpful this technique was in aiding in the restoration of the life of a young man named Alex that she knew.

Alex had two friends who borrowed his parent's car when they were out of town. Although Alex was not in the vehicle, his two friends were in a terrible car accident and died. Alex hated himself for allowing his friends to use the car. Prior to working with an EMDR specialist Alex life seemed hopeless. He had a marriage that disintegrated into divorce and he was unable to keep a job. He drank and struggled with other addictions most of the time. After working with an EMDR professional, he had gotten his life back. He happily remarried and enjoyed the birth of children, and he works at a fulfilling job.

"In 1987, psychologist Dr. Francine Shapiro made the chance observation that eye movements can reduce the intensity of disturbing thoughts, under certain conditions. Dr. Shapiro studied this effect scientifically, and in a 1989 issue of the *Journal of Traumatic Stress,* she reported success using EMDR to treat victims of trauma. Since then, EMDR has developed and evolved through the contributions of therapists and researchers all over the world. Today, EMDR is a set of standardized protocols that incorporates elements from many different treatment approaches."[5]

After Jennifer's phone call to my mom, I decided to seek out an EMDR therapist and found one through the Website, *www.emdria.org.* It is a Website that provides information on EMDR and therapists who are certified in the technique, but doesn't make referrals to specific EMDR therapists.

Sophie was a warm and compassionate therapist and very knowledgeable in her field of treating post-traumatic stress disorder. I appreciated that she often sought continued education and various certifications to increase her knowledge base in EMDR treatment. Over time we developed trust and I began to feel comfortable in opening up and sharing the painful process of recovery with her. I worked with Sophie extensively in ninety-minute sessions, sometimes twice a week, on the issue of grief and trauma. Over time, EMDR helped me to regain more control over my pain by permitting me to feel it in a non-threatening environment and release it safely.

Sophie not only helped me deal with the grieving process and trauma of Nathaniel's death, but she also helped me learn how to manage and keep a balanced lifestyle. During my time in therapy and through embracing and relying on my active faith life, I was able to get back to working more hours and enjoying many of my hobbies, such as singing in the choir, joining a book club and doing a little traveling. I guess you could say that after the four years of important time I spent with Sophie, she knew me better than almost anyone.

Sophie was on the witness stand for one minute, and was not asked one question by the pharmaceutical company's attorneys.

Into Hell Without A Warning

About a year before the trial, James and Peter sent a deposition via email for me to review. It was one of the last major depositions taken, although I did not know it at the time, because with major financial backing Charles and Susan had a tenacious way of overstaying their welcome in a person's life. It turned out to be a deposition of one of our expert witnesses. Dr. Simmons was a kind man that was an expert on amphetamine-induced psychosis. He worked on Nicholas's case as well as mine. I had met with Dr. Simmons many times before he was deposed, for both psychological testing, as well as for individual sessions. My mother, father, Cindy, Michael and I also met with a trauma specialist that Dr. Simmons observed while she worked with us for several sessions that incorporated the techniques of psychodrama as we retold the painful events of Nathaniel's and my accident.

Peter and James had invited me to attend Dr. Simmons's deposition. I intended to go, but got so sick when it was time for me to go that I missed it. Peter and James were forgiving, but thought it important enough to send to me as an attachment via email. When I received the deposition and began to print it out I felt shock and dread. Page after page after page began pouring out of the printer. It ended up being 450 pages. I remember saying to myself, "You mean all of this is because of my taking that little pill!" I wasn't sure what to do or what was expected of me.

As I began to read the first few pages I was horrified to read the web that was woven by the pharmaceutical company's attorneys. It was at this point I struggled to hope that there would be any justice seen for my son. It made me sick to my stomach because after reading only a few pages I knew how far they were willing to go to win. I sensed my blood beginning to boil and I immediately set their instrument of mass destruction down on the table.

I made what I felt then was the best decision for me after having sat through five-and-a-half years of endless depositions, freely giving hundreds upon hundreds of my signatures for release of document acquisitions, and the continuous answering of a barrage of interrogative questioning from the pharmaceutical company's attorneys. Enough was enough, and I chose not to give the company and their hired assassins the luxury of destroying the life of another person. I decided not to read this deposition. Because I'd been so willing to attend to and participate in everything else having to do with my case, I am not certain Peter and James realized this was how I felt about reading Dr. Simmons's deposition.

As the trial date grew closer, my weekly counseling sessions with Sophie had become more about lessons in survival and balancing the stress the trial placed on me. I never read Charles and Susan's strategy for my disposal. Nor did my attorneys prepare me for what lay ahead. How could they? As the trial date approached, the grief over my son's death seemed to pervade every minute. Midway through litigation I expected this would be the case. I felt all the pain and sadness of Nathaniel's death as if it had just happened. Right or wrong, what kept me going was my love for my son and the desire to help others avoid the terror we had been through. I was strengthened to move forward one small step at a time for one reason and one reason only—Nathaniel.

I was sent to the witness stand like a soldier to the front lines without a weapon or a shield, but only a prayer. I held tightly to my love for Nathaniel in my heart and my rosary clenched in my hand for what would not be a 45-minute time-frame as my attorneys supposed, but for the three longest hours of my life.

A Message From A Friend

Hi Dawn,

It was so good to hear from you. I was thinking of you this weekend, and I hope we can catch up in person, soon!

How in the world did they [the opposing attorneys] get that letter from St. Jude's. First of all, I can never thank you enough for defending me against those people that were attempting to defame my character.

Not only was that letter passionate, but eloquent and nothing but the truth! I can't believe that the "other side" of your court case has the audacity to attack you as a Christian, a mother, or a woman of faith!!!! It makes me sick to think that you have to endure that, as if you haven't been through enough already. I don't know if there's anything I can do, but I would love to tell people what a devoted Christian you are and what an amazing mother you were to Nathaniel. Those people haven't a clue as to your character, faith or integrity. You are in my prayers and I know that the truth will prevail.

As for me, things are good...

Love,

Gina

The letter Gina is talking about is one that I wrote during my employment as a Resource Teacher at St. Jude's Catholic School. During my employment at this school, a very unhappy person or persons had written and typed four separate anonymous letters, made copies and sent them to every parent in the school and every person who belonged to the very large parish community. They were sent out sporadically over a period of several months, and not one of them was signed. In these letters were written a host of false accusations, half truths and lies which attempted to defame the administration at the school. One person who was in the line of fire was my friend Gina. I had known Gina for years. She was one of the teens I had taught when I worked in youth ministry. I knew her character and accomplishments. Gina grew into a beautiful and brilliant young woman who was passionate about teaching. As a Resource Teacher I was able to observe her as she taught her students in the classroom.

In these letters she was accused of not having her credentials, which simply was not true. Not only was I hurting for Gina, but these letters caused such a ruckus in the school it was all the students could talk about. I wrote a letter meant only for the teachers, to rally us together. In it I quoted a verse from Genesis about the devil in a garden, who used language to deceive. I did not make thousands of copies but a few. I signed my name to it. Many people thanked me for writing the letter, saying I had the guts to write what they were feeling and thinking. The silence was broken.

After the principal's car got keyed, something even more dreadful happened. She received several death threats. When her children's lives were endangered she resigned. The new principal was a parent of one of the students at the school. When I went for review to renew my contract she said to me, "If it weren't for you things were going just fine!"

> *...and yet, amidst all my voicing and firm stance against what I feel is injustice, I am most difficult on myself, a task that has thankfully been tempered these years through the learning process that only hardcore experience can bring. I fall down, I get up, I fall down, I get up. I love the quote in the final Rocky [final I think], where Balboa is speaking to his downtrodden son about the toughness of the world and says: "It's not about how hard you get hit (because it's going to happen). It's about how hard you* ***get*** *hit and keep moving forward!"*

January 13, 2006

6:10 a.m.

I am in awe upon waking up this morning to have read in my Magnificat issue January 2006 the 13th, the day which I am to take the witness stand the following:

An Attitude Of Faith

History is not in the hands of the powers of darkness, chance, or human decisions alone. When evil energy that we see is unleashed, when Satan vehemently bursts in, when a multitude of scourges and ills surface, the Lord, the supreme arbiter of historical events, arises. He leads

> history wisely toward the dawn of the new heavens and the new earth...
>
> There is consequently a desire to reaffirm that God is not indifferent to human events but penetrates them, creating his own "ways" or, in other words, his effective plans and "deeds"...
>
> The nations must learn to "read" God's message in history. The adventure of humanity is not confused and meaningless, nor is it doomed, never to be appealed against or to be abused by the overbearing and the perverse...
>
> This attitude of faith leads men and women to recognize the power of God who works in history and thus to open themselves to feeling awe for the name of the Lord. In biblical language, in fact, this "fear" is not fright. It is recognition of the mystery of divine transcendence. Thus, it is at the root of faith and interwoven with love... As Saint Hilary of Poitiers, a fourth-century bishop, said: "All our fear is in love."[6]
>
> —Pope Benedict XVI

Three hours long.

The Pharmaceutical Company's Deception

During one of my moments on the witness stand the pharmaceutical company's attorney asked me if I had ever dated George, to which I emphatically answered, No! He continued, then why was it in Dr. Martin's records? My response was that if that was how Dr. Martin interpreted our relationship, then that was his interpretation. With George's incessant visits at the house came his offer to drop me off at my appointments. Dr. Martin had written a side note, as any doctor might, not an in-depth assessment of a relationship, because there simply wasn't anything more than a platonic friendship.

"The only normal people are the ones
you don't know very well."
—Alfred Adler

5:30 p.m.

Our side rested it's case today. The judge denied the pharmaceutical company's motion for directed verdict. The jury will decide that question he said. Defense goes on 1/30/06, and should last about a week. James and Peter told me they thought I'd be on the stand for a half an hour to forty five minutes at the most. The pharmaceutical company had me on the witness stand for three hours. I am wiped out but I held strong. That was for you my sweet son and it was worth every dreadful, painful second.

An email sent to my address book:

Dawn Marie did a FABULOUS job on the witness stand. They have tried to smear her so badly throughout this case, and she stood up for herself and for Nathaniel. They were slimy; she was a lady. We are very proud of her!

James

8:45 pm

I overheard shop talk between the attorneys while I was at dinner with my parents. They said Charles was a pharmacist before becoming an attorney. Terrific, I'm up against the devil himself. No wonder he is so good at the art of medicinal manipulation. What a nightmare. Nonetheless, God permitted me to learn of this now, perhaps knowing this I would have quit a long time ago. God's timing is perfect. Father, please help me see your will in all of this.

While I worked with Dr. Martin he had referred me to a psychiatrist, Dr. Kingston, who made the recommendation that I take medication as I worked through my issues of deep sorrow regarding Nathaniel's abrupt passing. Dr. Kingston was a brilliant, faith-filled doctor whose compassion and patience with my going on and off many medications due to my fear of "losing my mind" at the sign of the slightest side effect was heroic. He hung in there with me and never bailed on me, to which I am forever grateful. This was a treacherous period of my life, where I worked through the ins and outs of trauma. Charles used this to his advantage in courtroom dramatics. He delivered a list of medications to the jury which I had taken either long before or after Nathaniel died, NOT during the time frame of our car accident.

I flew back to Arizona. The trial would resume in one week. My attorneys felt I had done a good job on the stand. The longest week of my life was ahead of me, yet God, as always, had a way of weaving streams of hope in the darkest of times. During that week I was reintroduced to an amazing man, Robert Roeder, who would one day become my husband. "For I know well the plans I have in mind for you, declares the Lord. Plans for your welfare not for woe; plans to give you a future full of hope." (Jer 29:11)

The first time I met Robert was several years earlier when 20 of us from a Catholic singles group arranged to go to Carlsbad, California for a Memorial Day weekend getaway. I didn't know Robert very well because he was new to the group, but I do remember his dead-on Dr. Phil impersonation that made me and everyone else laugh hysterically. It was a memorable weekend where everyone, in large and small groups, would dine, dance, sing, attend concerts and enjoy the beach. I bumped into Robert several times over that weekend, yet we didn't get a chance to talk much because we were heading in different directions. Two years later Robert and I reconnected, and it happened to be over the weekend of my one-week off between the trial.

I spent most of my time that week resting. The mental energy expended during the course of the previous week was profound. I was present for every minute of the trial and the sense of sitting on the sidelines while your life is being analyzed and scrutinized in the minutest of details felt daunting. I felt as though I was stripped of everything dear to me and totally naked before all. I decided I would get as much rest as possible and I replenished myself through time with friends and being silent in the Adoration Chapel.

In his book *The Inner Voice of Love*, Henry J. Nouwen offers suggestions for working around your abyss. He states, "There are two extremes to avoid: being completely absorbed in your pain and being distracted by so many things that you stray far away from the wound you want to heal."[7] I knew the importance of allowing myself to feel all the emotions that would come up during the trial, in a constructive way, if I were going to survive it. It was a second-by-second choice not to be absorbed in pain and the pharmaceutical company's accusations. I did light therapeutic stretches which were very helpful for releasing back pain and strain after the car accident. I took hot baths. I spoke with loved ones on the phone. I listened to inspirational tapes. I took walks in the neighborhood and brought my dog to the park. I was in the middle of a courtroom marathon and I needed to keep my endurance up as much as possible and...I prayed.

When the weekend before returning for trial arrived, I decided on Friday to attend the Divine Mercy Mass and prayer celebration at Saint Ann's Church in the town of Gilbert. I believed it would be a wonderful way of entering and centering on peace-filled prayer and meditation to give me additional strength and focus for my continuing journey in the courtroom. Robert was there along with several other good friends from around the valley. After the beautiful celebration ended, a small group of us went to Applebee's® Restaurant for a bite to eat. Robert came along. This was the first time I'd ever had the chance to sit across from him at the same table. When he spoke he told jokes and laughed with friends and I found that he made me laugh again as he had done years earlier.

But this time as he entertained everyone, I couldn't seem to take my eyes off of him. I was struck by his kind-heartedness and the genuine love and concern he expressed for his friends. *What a great guy*, I thought to myself, as the evening seemed to come to an end too quickly.

One of the beautiful things about a church community is that there is always something to be involved with in ministry, and along with this comes invaluable friendships. One of the more challenging aspects of the investment in ministry and its friendships is time management—being able to prioritize what events one can and cannot attend out of the many events that are available. But over the weekend before trial I cut myself some slack because I needed community and my friends, and so I decided to attend a birthday party on Saturday that was being thrown for one of the most selfless guys in the singles group, Joseph.

Due to a prior commitment, I ended up coming a little late to Joseph's dinner party, which was being held at Macayo's Mexican Restaurant in Mesa. When I got there, there was a large group of people sitting at a very long table and I wondered if there would be any room for me. There just happened to be one seat available and it was right next to Robert. I happily sat down. We talked some more and found that we owned the same print of a painting and that we both held a fond memory of it and of its artist, Pierre-Auguste Renoir. We reminisced at having seen the original "Luncheon of the Boating Party" painting at the Phoenix Art Museum a year earlier. We expressed our awe over its size, depth, personality, dimension, color and the joy it brought us to see it in person. *Hmm,* I thought to myself, *mutual friends, mutual faith, mutual interests.*

After the evening was over I remember feeling a sense of contentment, having enjoyed the moments I spent with Robert and learning more about him. *Could I be falling in love?* I wondered, and quickly dismissed the thought. This was crazy, he was going to school full time and working full time and I was in the middle of the fight of my life. *Nah!* I thought to myself—it's just not possible.

Sunday evening Robert and I would meet again when my dear friend Cathy surprised me with a birthday celebration at Nellos Pizzeria in Old Town Scottsdale. What a blessed evening to be surrounded by friends who showered me with much love and support. When Robert arrived at the door I remember being glad to see him. He made his way through the crowd and grabbed a seat across from where I sat. Once again I enjoyed his pleasantries and humor. I left that evening thinking to myself, *this guy is incredible!*

Yet sadness quickly returned to my heart. It was time to return back east to face the pharmaceutical companies defense. One again I was reminded of God's love and mercy, and once again it came through Saint Padre Pio of Pietrelcina.

> *Has the Lord not told us that He is faithful and promised never to allow us to be vanquished? God is faithful, and He will not let you be tempted beyond your strength, but with the temptation will also provide the way of escape, that you may be able to endure it.*
>
> *How could you persuade yourself of anything else? Isn't our good God far above anything we can conceive? Isn't He more interested than we are in our salvation? How many times has He not given us proof of this? How many victories have you not gained over your very powerful enemies and over yourself, through the divine assistance, without which you would inevitably have been crushed?*
>
> *Let us consider Jesus' love for us and His concern for our well-being and then let us be at peace. Let us not doubt that He will invariably assist us with more than Fatherly care against all our enemies. If it were left only to ourselves to remain on our feet, we should never be able to do it. At the first breath of air we should fall down and certainly have no hope of rising again. The more numerous your enemies become, the more you ought to abandon yourself with complete trust in the Lord. He*

will always sustain you with His powerful arm so that you may not stumble.

Before the Lord abandons us, we should have to abandon Him: in a word, we should first have to close the door of our heart to Him, and even then, how many times does He not stretch out his Hand to us to arrest our headlong dash toward the precipice? How many times, when we had abandoned Him, has He not readmitted us to His loving embrace!

How good our God is! Blessed forever be His hand which many times alleviates our sufferings and marvelously heals our incurable wounds.[8]

Back In Session—Hypocrisy Abounds

When the pharmaceutical company's team entered the courtroom and took their positions, Susan dramatically slammed two large stacks of paper down on the corner of their counsel table as if to profess the drug company's safety measures. I thought to myself, *It's only paper and God only knows the quantity of red tape this company has logged in Washington.*

What I witnessed the following days as the defense made its case against us was that their strategy was not about sharing the many supposed studies they had completed and submitted to the FDA on the safety of their drug, but instead, it was a direct attack and assault on my character, because that was all they had! In addition, their expert witness's testimonies only convinced me all the more I was doing the right thing, for I felt if this company was willing to stoop to this level of hypocrisy, what more damage were they capable of doing?

One of their expert witnesses was a retired senior employee of the Food and Drug Administration. After a monologue defending the pharmaceutical company, my attorney, James, brought to everyone's attention a paper the retired employee had written in his last year while still employed for the FDA. It was, of all things, about why the FDA should not collaborate with the pharmaceutical industry because it was *a conflict of interest!*

Another expert witness for the pharmaceutical company was the forensic psychiatrist with whom I had spent a few moments, compared to the many hours I had spent with Sophie. But he was a forensic psychiatrist paid $60,000 by the pharmaceutical company for his services. This was the same team of "experts" who gave Nicholas a diagnosis without ever having seen him. The forensic psychiatrist's accusation against me was that I had "false memory retrieval" regarding the accident. I will address this issue later.

The Accident

When it came time for both sides to argue over the actual day of Nathaniel's death and the accident that killed him, I told my attorneys as I had before that I had no memories of the crash—of either the impact or what lead up to it. There would be no way I was going to put myself through Charles's PowerPoint extravaganza of accident pictures and his interpretation of what caused Nathaniel to die that day. I felt God had spared me the horror of what it would have been to see my poor son's badly bruised and bleeding body, although I later had to experience the agony of seeing him on the day of his funeral, which created in me a feeling of pain and helplessness I would never forget. James walked up to the judge to ask if I could leave the courtroom during Charles's PowerPoint presentation of the accident. Charles quickly raced to his side. What the jurors were about to witness I could hardly imagine, because Charles had a thirst for blood and that was what they were going to see. When James returned to the counsel table with the judge's permission, I left the courtroom.

Diabolical Evidence

Then it came time for the reading of George's deposition. The young man chosen by the pharmaceutical company to read George's deposition made a pit stop at our counsel table before taking the witness stand. He leaned over and pushed between James and Jason and grabbed an unopened water bottle from our table and cracked it open on his way to the stand.

The day that George was deposed I was not present. For my safety, my attorneys did not insist I attend this one. Nor had I read Dr. Simmons's 450-page deposition that had been sent to me. So I had no idea to what extent George had lied under oath. It was unconscionable. My father had said I simply would rather not look at the bad in a person and what this company used as their main defense was bad to the core. George had made so many blatant and false claims that the pharmaceutical company was able to justify their own falsehoods. George testified that he came with me into the doctor's office while I was seen by him. BIG FAT LIE!

When I had my visit with Dr. Byrnes, the doctor who George recommended, I felt I had what was a thorough appointment. I discussed with him my struggles with paying attention during high school and college, and my having gone through extensive testing at the clinic that specialized in diagnosing ADD. Dr. Byrnes recommended for my treatment the prescription medication at that time. I asked him what the side effects were. He told me they were minor, such as possible dry mouth and constipation. He told me it was a "class two" medication and that because of this, he needed to see me in one week. I asked him what "class two" meant and he said that it was regulated by the federal government along with other popular medications to treat ADD. I felt a false sense of security thinking it was a good thing that the medication was regulated by the federal government.

Dr. Byrnes prescribed a low dose and said that he would raise it to its level of efficacy (a term used by the medical industry to describe when a medication reaches its level of effectiveness) after two weeks, depending on how I was doing. I left his office and made an appointment to see him in one week. I went to the local pharmacy near my home and was not given any different information from the pharmacist about the potential side effects of the medication.

I had arranged for time off from work for my second appointment, and while I was *en route* to Dr. Byrnes office I received a phone call from his secretary. She called to inform me that he had a family emergency out of town and would be unable to see me that day, and that I needed to reschedule. I immediately set up a second appointment for a few days later.

When I got into my car to drive for my second appointment, I decided I had better call ahead of time to make certain the doctor was back in his office. His secretary answered the phone and told me once again he would be unable to see me. It was at this time I became a little frantic. Although I knew I was taking a low dose, I felt uncomfortable being on a new medication without proper supervision. I immediately called the ADD clinic I had received the diagnosis from and they gave me a recommendation to see Dr. Jennings, who specialized in this field. I had an appointment within a couple of days.

Prior to my appointment, the clinic had faxed all of my records to Dr. Jennings's office, which he used to make an assessment. He decided I continue taking the low dose for my first few weeks as he assessed my progress. I had a good rapport with Dr. Jennings and had no problems with his office in setting up additional appointments for my care. After the second month, Dr. Jennings increased my dosage to its level of efficacy. It was at that time I began to take a turn for the worse.

As George's deposition was read, Charles made absolutely certain he selected the precise false accusations to be read. George claimed he worked for our family business but he never stepped foot in our shop. He attacked me on my ability as a mother, falsely saying that I left my son on a curb unattended. He said my mother was an alcoholic, which is one of the biggest jokes, as she dislikes alcohol abuse and made a choice very early in her life not to allow its negative influence upon her as it had in the lives of one of her dearest loved ones. And, as I already mentioned, he claimed he was in the room with me when I was being seen by the doctor. BFL

George also attacked my faith, saying it was not genuine. Thankfully, James was able to make a significant point. He had their hired assassin read from the deposition a comment that George made, which highlighted his own delusional character. George commented on the intense emotion he had felt when I stopped by the home of a sick friend to say a quick prayer for them. George said that when I prayed for this friend, he "feared the demons would come out of this person and enter him." Who was calling who psychotic!

George's "Healing"

I felt pretty stupid for having believed George. I punished myself with grief and guilt, saying I should have known better, that I was so gullible to have believed him.

He said that the reason he was in a wheelchair was due to a car accident. He told me conflicting stories about how the accident occurred so I did not know for sure what really happened. He had a therapist that came to his home for physical therapy sessions. I remember him complaining one day about the insurance plan. It was shortly after that complaint he received his remarkable "healing."

Who was I to judge, I had felt at the time. I had witnessed miracles abroad and in the states. I was happy for him and explained my own hope to find a good doctor for the treatment of my ADD as it was my desire to go back to graduate school and provide a better life for my son. He claimed he too had ADD and that he knew a doctor who could treat mine—Dr. Byrnes.

Hearing George's deposition being read I wanted to die. The pharmaceutical company was trying to make it look like George and I had a romantic history. George went right along with them.

How terrible I felt. I had taken advice from a psychopathic liar. At first I felt naive and stupid. Then after being sad for a while I got angry. George was hung up on ruining other people's lives instead of taking responsibility for his own. How funny; since this company seemed hell bent on doing the same. Nonetheless, George was not a part of my life at the time I made my appointment with Dr. Jennings as I stated earlier. The pharmaceutical company went all out to block critical evidence. With all the chaos and cloud of confusion the company mustered up in their incessant attacks on my character, and with Sophie not being permitted to speak, Dr. Jennings and his wonderful treatment of me never got mentioned during trial. I now realized why it was that the company fought so vehemently to keep Sophie quiet. She knew the truth about George, she knew the truth about Dr. Jennings, and they were terrified of her.

The "Grand" Finale

The company's reading of George's deposition meant I had witnessed the level to which they had all sunk. Although I sat through hours and hours of their assaults and insults, I decided to preserve my sanity during the last deposition. This was to be Susan's reading of Dr. Crawford's deposition.

I recalled a conversation that I had when George was at my parents' home, shortly after my release from the hospital as I grappled with my pain. One year before Nathaniel's and my accident I was seeing a female doctor named Dr. Crawford. How curious, I thought that hers was the last deposition. During my visits with Crawford, she told me she had been involved in a lawsuit regarding a medication. I remember how nervy and on edge she appeared.

Dr. Crawford was someone I saw when my husband Bill and his cousin Phil had made some very irresponsible decisions regarding their addictions and Bill's and my financial situation. Unfortunately, I had become accustomed at this time to Dr. Crawford's secretary's reminder calls for my appointments, and I did not received two calls and missed two appointments, which prompted Dr. Crawford to end our sessions. By the time the pharmaceutical company took her deposition, Dr. Crawford had moved out of state. I did not attend her deposition.

Recalling that George was present when I mentioned Dr. Crawford's name, I knew this deposition was going to be ugly. As Susan seized the deposition and rounded their table, she smirked to the jury before approaching the witness stand. I appreciated my prior action.

Upon entering the courtroom, I jammed two contraptions into my ears that I had made out of spittle and toilet paper during a quick bathroom break, and I plugged them up! I had listened to hour after hour of bull____. I would not give Susan or her company the satisfaction of seeing me squirm because I knew I would have screamed from the top of my lungs, lies, lies, lies, lies, lies! Instead I refused to listen to them, as I knew that grave damage to truth had already been done.

When Susan was finished, court was adjourned. The pharmaceutical company had succeeded in bringing it down to the level of a battle between a doctor and a patient. Once again they shrugged their responsibility to give these very doctors the vital information they needed to be of greater assistance in caring for their patients by giving them crucial and critical knowledge about their prescription drugs.

Friday arrived and it was time for closing arguments. I overheard Charles at lunch say that he planned to compare the prescribed medication to Gerber baby food in his closing arguments. He said it was only fair, because its maker was from another country, just as the pharmaceutical company was. His heartless, low-life ways knew no bounds. I thought he was a pansy to resort to such a statement.

Charles greased up his high-tech computer and put his presentation screen on the courtroom floor. It took him about an hour to get his equipment the way he wanted it. He was meticulous about the lighting, the sound, the location, the height, the distance, the cords, the plugs. At last, he was ready—for his final kill.

His closing began with a list of medications that I had taken during my lifetime, some of which were accurate and some of which I had never seen nor heard of. He spoke of my employment history at St. Jude's and his claim of "psychosis" that he said was evident because I wrote Scripture in a letter at a Catholic Christian school. He said I was irresponsible, not a good mother and that I came from a challenged family. Who doesn't have challenges in their family?! He accused me of a suicide attempt and of killing my child.

When it came time for James to close arguments he asked for all of Charles's technical equipment to be taken down. Once it was finally removed, he placed a picture of Nathaniel and me by the witness stand and he spoke briefly about the fact that Nicholas's case never got an opportunity for civil trial. Then he did something amazing. He got down on the floor of the courtroom with two model cars. While moving the cars forward on the courtroom floor as if on the road, he explained how the primary witnesses in car number two testified how car number one, my car, wavered and weaved on the road as if the person in the car was not in control. He continued with more examples of eyewitness testimony.

James did a great job conveying the very painful set of circumstances, which he knew I was hearing for the first time. What he made apparent in his closing was that the driver of car number one was perilously out of control of her vehicle and was an accident waiting to happen.

Nathaniel's Second Birthday

A few months before I began taking the prescription medication, I had the joy of celebrating Nathaniel's birthday on November 10, 1999. Once again I made him a special birthday cake. I decided to make this an annual event that would be my unique way of expressing to him how much I loved him.

As I tried to think of what design to make the cake I thought about the things that Nathaniel enjoyed. He loved the "Veggie Tale" video series. I remember fondly how he danced with glee, and be-bopped to the "Veggie Tale" intro song, where Larry the Cucumber played his tuba and Bob the Tomato and veggie friends burst into a symphonic melody that celebrated the life and mysteries of vegetable being.

Nathaniel adored water. He could not seem to get enough of the feel, swish and sounds of water flowing, dripping, sloshing and swirling everywhere from the fountain at my folks' business that stands at the entrance to the Scottsdale Design Center, where Marco Draperies and Interior's remained one of the sole tenants for more than twenty two years. He ran around the fountain a hundred times, oblivious of onlookers and my watchful presence, as he laughed and galloped and reveled in the fountain's multi-faceted aqua starburst display.

He loved his play pool and he displayed no fear when being placed in his inflated seated inner tube in the big people's pool. And puddles, did he enjoy puddles! He would stand in awe and exultation of the waters' sensation under his feet and would clap at the waves and ripples he could create with the smallest of movements.

Nathaniel loved his grandparents and his Uncle Tony, who taught him how to position himself in a three-point stance and ready himself for having been born into a football-loving, Arizona Cardinal season-ticket holding family.

Nathaniel loved Christmas and was blessed to have met Santa Clause three times from his birth onward, thanks to the loving gesture of our friends, May and Jerry Polk—Jerry would mysteriously disappear when Santa arrived at our door.

And Nathaniel was mesmerized by his favorite DVD, which featured the Three Tenors. I was amazed at my son's captivation with Jose Carreras, Placido Domingo and Luciano Pavarotti. Being a teacher and having studied child development, I marveled at how a two-year-old little boy could stand and listen to almost the entire DVD! When Pavarotti would sing in his broad-chested, crystal-clear, rich and beautiful tenor voice, Nathaniel became a mini Pavarotti, standing tippy-toed and mimicking in motion, swaying his arms broadly, with eyes opened wide. He would coo and hum, opening his mouth as large as his favorite tenor, and out of him came the greatest expressions of joy and happiness the world could possibly contain. He was in ecstasy and so was I, in embracing the marvel before me, the littlest tenor, Nathaniel Joseph.

As one could see, I had many choices from which to choose to make his cake, from a football, to a Veggie Tale character, to a water fountain to a musical note. Since I was reading him a dinosaur book he enjoyed at bedtime, I chose to surprise him with a big green dinosaur!

This cake took me several hours to make and I enjoyed every second of creating it!

Sixth Sorrow
John 19:27

"Behold, your Mother"

Nowhere in the Bible is it recorded that when Jesus was taken down from the cross He was placed in the arms of His mother. Yet the Bible states that she was there, and as common sense tells any of us who are parents, the first thing we would do instinctively upon seeing our child injured, or as in this sad case deceased, would be to run to them, with no power on earth being able to stand in the way of our holding the one who we bore and raised. No one will ever be able to tell me that Mary did not hold her Son, Jesus, in her arms the day He died.

Michelangelo made several Pietas, his white marble masterpieces of the Mother of God, holding in her arms the lifeless body of Jesus after He was taken down from the cross. One of Michelangelo's Pietas resides at the Vatican in Rome. But this particular Pieta was not his favorite. The one that he found most profound while sculpting it was the depiction of Jesus laying in the arms of his faceless mother, because Michelangelo wondered how it could ever be possible to expect to know the pain the Mother of God felt the day her Son Jesus died, and what she felt when He was placed in her arms.

...and his mother kept all these things in her heart.[1]

Six

The Verdict

February 3, 2006

Dear Friends, at Dawn Marie's request I am writing to advise you of the jury's verdict against us at 3:05 p.m. today. The first question was whether the prescribed medication was defective or "unreasonably dangerous," because of the pharmaceutical company's failure to warn. The jury answered "No."

What this makes clear is that, although Dawn was attacked mercilessly by the pharmaceutical company, in fact we lost on the issue that focused on the company, NOT Dawn. It is small consolation, but some yet.

Thanks to all of you who have held us up with your prayers throughout this ordeal. We needed them...and for the next few days we will continue to need them even more.

We are low. Very low. However, we are comforted to know that all of you are thinking of us. God bless.

James and Peter,
Joe and Catherine
and Dawn Marie

I was told to remove *www.Nathaniellives.com* from the Internet.

My father and I wondered, if we had no knowledge of our family and our tragedy and we had been sitting on the jury these two weeks receiving the defamatory information, lack of permissible information and misinformation the jurors received, would we have rendered the same vote?

Nathaniel's Merciful Heart

I will never forget the moment of compassion Nathaniel demonstrated while we were in the prayer garden at the Evangelical Sisterhood of Mary in Phoenix, Arizona. As I had often liked to go to the prayer garden before Nathaniel was born, now that things had fallen into a nice routine, I decided it was time to take him there. He was about one year old.

He instantly fell in love with Canaan in the Desert, as it is also called, and with eagerness he began his first steps in the direction of the large stone cylinder fountain. He smiled and laughed, joyfully exploring every inch of the outer rim of the fountain that gushed and cascaded heaps of crystal-clear water like a geyser from its top. We spent much time delighting in the water, and I enjoyed watching Nathaniel laugh while we playfully splashed in the well.

After some time, I took Nathaniel by the hand and walked toward the shaded area at the entrance of the garden where there was a wooden bench, and a four-foot-by-four-foot clay plaque with a sculpted image of Jesus slumped over a large stone, depicting the Agony of Our Lord in the Garden of Gethsemane. I sat on the bench for a bit while Nathaniel explored his immediate surroundings, the lush desert greenery. As I sat briefly meditating and sharing in this special moment with Nathaniel, I reflected upon what Jesus suffered for us. I said a prayer of thanksgiving and blessing for my son as Nathaniel wandered his way closer to the sculpture. As I finished my prayer, Nathaniel did something that stunned me, because this was his first time here. He walked to the side of the clay plaque where Jesus was, laid his little palm on Jesus's back and began stroking and patting his back. The scripture "bid the little children to come to Me for theirs is the Kingdom of Heaven," rang louder than life for me that day.

Seventh Sorrow
Mark 15:46

"a stone against the entrance of the tomb"

I wonder what Mary felt the day they placed her son Jesus in the tomb and rolled a stone over it to cover the entrance. I know what I felt the day of Nathaniel's burial. As the dirt was being thrown onto the casket of my son I wanted to leap into the hole and be buried with him.

Tortured anguish Mother deep entwine
The Sword now passed thrust into Thine
A Sorrow fathomed ne'r to attain
Death's loss brought Life through Love's sweet gain.
—D.M. Roeder

The most beautiful people we have known are those who have known defeat, known suffering, known struggle, known loss, and have found their way out of the depths. These persons have an appreciation, a sensitivity and an understanding of life that fills them with compassion, gentleness, and a deep loving concern. Beautiful people do not just happen.[1]
—Elisabeth Kübler-Ross

and the angel of the Lord declared unto
Mary you shall bear a son...[2]

Her response:

YES.

Seven

The Burial Of My Dream

Immediately after the verdict was read my entire team of attorneys, my family members and I rushed into the side counsel room and closed the door. Quizzically, the pharmaceutical company's team immediately dispersed as they'd accomplished their dirty deed, but I doubt it was done dirt cheap. When I sat down, I thanked my team for their enormous effort. They had become my family for the five-and-a-half years I had come to know them. They are incredible men and women of honor and integrity. They were hurting for me and my family. I could see it in their eyes. I later learned that James rode back to his home with Joseph and their equipment, a nineteen-hour drive he made instead of taking his scheduled flight home.

I was proud to be represented by these individuals. After our good-byes, deep sadness enveloped my soul. With the reading of the verdict I experienced the burial of my dreams of justice for Nathaniel. I was crushed.

The following is an email sent to me by my dear friend Shannon:

Dawn Marie,

I am soooo sorry it's early Saturday, the day after the verdict, and I haven't yet gotten to talk to you because my son and I have been sick.

I just read Jason's, James's and Peter's emails. Wow. I am in awe of the emotion, the depth of caring and the sense of truly fighting for JUSTICE that yours and Nathaniel's case has inspired in countless numbers of people across the country and beyond. I can only imagine the heartbreak you must be feeling now, and were feeling the moment the jury's decision was read. You knew it would take a miracle, although God specializes in those! But the jury, the way the count was worded, did not provide justice in that courtroom. Although it would have been the most comforting outcome for you to have heard that the pharmaceutical company had been forced to take some responsibility, that apparently was not God's will. Maybe through this setback, your voice will only grow stronger. You, along with those who fought this battle tooth and nail, will speak at every opportunity, so others may not suffer the same tragedy. People like me and all your friends and family who support you will also speak, so your voice, and Nathaniel's sweet voice, will never be silenced. Sometimes it's when we don't get the outcome we so dearly needed, we find other ways to get our message across. I can guarantee whether it's this prescribed medication, or another situation where a company is acting unethical, I am going to spread your story so others are aware. This can be more damaging to the pharmaceutical company than they may think. Their Judgment Day will come, when individuals will be held accountable.

Dawn, this outcome does not affect the way I believe you or believe in you. If anything, I know that you love your son Nathaniel so deeply that you were able to show tremendous dignity and grace to those who so horribly attacked you. You should be proud of yourself, just as we are of you. I know I'm speaking for many, many people, and I have no doubt that I am speaking the truth. However, your heart, your mind, your emotions, your self-esteem, your faith are undoubtedly in tatters right now, especially as you begin to come out of the fog that has been the trial. Thing is, those shreds of love, faith and hope can be mended into the whole and beautiful tapestry that is God's will for you. I pray that you can open the fists you have used to fight the pharmaceutical company and let God's merciful hands lovingly lead you into a place where He can have some one-one-one time with his precious daughter Dawn Marie. He wants so badly to help you heal, so you may go on and answer His next call—whatever that may be. Trust that He will comfort you and heal you before sending anything more to test your strength, and, more importantly, your faith. You are a LIVING EXAMPLE of trusting in God's love for us, no matter what.

Please remember, this very, very difficult phase of your life is over, and now you have earned the right to take however much time YOU NEED to heal so that you may be healthy to go on to the next phase. YOU DESERVE IT.

Thank you, Dawn Marie, for allowing me to share in this very important process, and for showing me what it means to be a loving mother, daughter, sister, and chosen daughter of God's.

I love you!!!!!
Shannon

I was deeply moved by Shannon's letter. The loving and tender words she expressed, her support and the support of my family, friends and community, held me up strong after the trial was over. I cried many tears, but in them I was consoled as I knew in my heart I gave it everything I had to try to help protect other people. It took me a while to feel this way because it did feel as if I had lost my son again, but I could look in the mirror at night and feel good about myself. I stood for change and there was nothing in the world that felt better than giving my life for something greater than myself—for standing in the gap for somebody else.

A time to heal, as Shannon expressed, was definitely what I needed, but it would not be long before shock and frustration would once again set in. Within six days of our losing the case, the FDA recommended placing the strongest warnings on this prescription medication as well as similar ADHD medications. This proved that the pharmaceutical company's statements about knowing "all there was to know" about their prescribed medication was, as James put it, "complete bullshit."

Hearing this news release only one week after our losing verdict brought up in me some very strong feelings. Before feeling the major emotions of anger and disgust, I felt disrespected, disregarded, demeaned and betrayed. I felt a strong betrayal by the very country I loved and would give my life to protect. I felt broken trust in the depths of my heart over our justice system and who or what exactly was running our country.

In his book *Bold Love*, Dr. Dan B. Allender made an important point about the topic of revenge.

> Vengeance, at times, can be illegitimate, but it is not inherently wrong. Vengeance is part of the character of God and is not in contradiction with His love and mercy. Revenge involves a desire for justice. It is the intense wish to see ugliness destroyed, wrongs righted, and beauty restored. It is as inherent to the human soul as a desire for loveliness...
>
> If vengeance is inherently perverse, then God is wrong for claiming it as His domain.[1]

As my dad and I said during a break in the courtroom as the dynamics unfolded, it was obvious the company made it all about the issue of money, but in the course of the five-and-a-half years I had known my attorneys, I had never once asked them about anything having to do with the issue of money. At one point my dad wanted to scream and shout in the courtroom at the pharmaceutical company and its cohort, "Here's all the money we have, you give us back our Nathaniel and we'll call it even!" It took everything I had to calm my father down. Perhaps I should have let him vent.

Why was I attacked on the issue of my motherhood through George's deposition in which he said I was careless with Nathaniel? Because George was a pathological liar and willing to go to ANY lengths to see a person destroyed. Dr. Byrnes, who had testified on George's behalf during his custody trial, had several medical malpractice suits already filed against him. In addition, the Arizona Board of Medical Examiners had taken disciplinary action against him for self-medicating and other failures with patients. Dr. Byrnes had so many inaccuracies and blatant lies in his documents, which included altering my medical file, claiming that I missed FIVE appointments! I kept trying to tell Peter and James, this was not good and that the pharmaceutical company was going to try to make me look like a flake or something worse. Unfortunately, the company succeeded in getting the jury to go against us. Peter and I discussed at one point that it seemed Dr. Byrnes was not just George's doctor but his drug lord. What a horrible situation I was thrust into by the Byrnes/George alliance during the trial. It was as if the pharmaceutical company, George and Dr. Byrnes all came from the same vile root.

Why was I attacked on the issue of abortion when the world and our government say the fetus is not a child? Because it was a grievous wrong. I accepted my responsibility for my bad decision many years ago and ran to God in repentance. I made the necessary changes to see that it never happened again. I gave life during a strained marriage—the best choice I ever made was saying yes to Nathaniel. No regrets, but that of taking their prescription medication.

Why was I attacked about my faith and told it wasn't genuine? Because I am passionate about my relationship with God and not afraid to say so.

Where has the responsibility to warn the general public of potential dangers gone, FDA? Pharmaceutical industry, I ask you the same thing. Where has the responsibility to get important information to consumers gone?

Shortly after my failed attempts to get any decent or respectable response from the FDA regarding my reaction to the medication and Nathaniel's death and after I heard the news of Nicholas Jenkins's trial getting thrown out, I sent several emails in response to these decisions, including a typed and postal mailed letter to President George W. Bush:

> *Dear Mr. President,*
>
> *First I want to thank you and let you know that despite everything our nation is currently enduring I am grateful we have a man of dignity in the Oval Office. I am a member of the Presidential Prayer Team and receive their weekly emails and I pray for you often. You do in many ways bear the weight of the world on your shoulders. I pray for your continued wisdom, courage and strength. I also pray for you to know that you do not carry this cross alone and that many, many love, support and pray for you and your family daily.*
>
> *I know that with all you are currently enduring in trying to keep things aligned abroad of which I'm greatly appreciative, some of the important happenings on the home front may not capture your attention, which is understandable. I am here to share with you my story and the story of others who have been engaged in a war not by choice but out of necessity. It's a war which I have been thrust yet now actively choose to be engaged in so that others be spared the nightmare my family had to endure.*
>
> *In the year 2000, on the day March 18th I was in a horrible car accident in which my only two year old son Nathaniel died. At the time of the accident I was taking a medication prescribed by my doctor that I thought was going to help me in my studies at the graduate level. This medication was for the treatment of Attention Deficit Disorder, a diagnosis I received several years before. I had*

what is called a drug-induced psychosis while on this medication. Basically, I lost the faculties of my mind and thought I was seeing and hearing things not in reality and in this confusion I was involved in a horrible traffic collision of which Nathaniel didn't survive. In my research on the history of this particular medication of which thousands and possibly millions of children are taking daily I have come to find that...(due to legal reasons I am not permitted to include the following three sentences which regarded information on the NDA New Drug Application for the prescription medication because Nicholas's case never made it to civil trial).

Why I am telling you this is because currently a judicial decision has been made that I fear will not curtail tragic happenings as mine and Nicholas's but foster them by protecting those institutions and persons of greater wealth and power, namely the pharmaceutical industries and that the average person sitting in the doctors office with a right to know will not be given important information that is vital to his or her ability to make a sound decision regarding their own health care.

As you can tell I'm extremely passionate about this because an innocent and precious child's life was lost and I grieve immensely for the outcome of this judicial decision because it does not protect those who can not speak for themselves and by this I mean the thousands and possibly millions of children being given this drug by very well meaning parents, because their protectors namely their parents have not been given right and proper information.

Enclosed is a press release of the judges decision given by my attorneys who are as yourself men of honor and dignity else I be represented by anyone less I would not have the courage to stand and fight for what I strongly believe in.

God bless you and thank you for taking the time to read this letter.

Sincerely,
Dawn Marie

I received a response eight months later but the President's office did not respond. The letter was forwarded to another department. I received a letter from the Food and Drug Administration, saying thanks for the letter, sorry about your child, and here's information about our MedWatch program. What an insult! I had already contacted their MedWatch program and now had a total of four thank you letters. Surely, the response to this letter should have acknowledged my previous contacts. Basically, this late response did nothing to convince me of the adequacy or competence of the agency and industries involved.

As I asked earlier, what happened to the responsibility to warn, FDA? Where IS the responsibility to warn, pharmaceutical industry? I believe I was attacked so mercilessly and so vehemently by the pharmaceutical company because *they could*. Because the working relationship between the Food and Drug Administration and the pharmaceutical industry was muddled and broken. What about this company's opportunity to warn consumers after they learned that Nicholas's daughter Tara died? As I mentioned earlier, the pharmaceutical company sent a letter out to all of their doctors and distributors when their chemical factory had a fire, assuring the continuation of the manufacturing of their product. Wasn't a child more important than a product? The criminal trial decided so in Nicholas's case. Even the vice president of marketing accepted responsibility for this potentially drastic side effect. Shouldn't this vital information have been put in a letter and sent to distribution centers and doctors?

Oh forgive me, I forgot...Nicholas's case never made it to civil trial. It got thrown out!!

In Robert Jeffress's book, *When Forgiveness Doesn't Make Sense*, he comments on the difference between revenge and restitution:

> Revenge is the desire to see my offender suffer for the pain he has inflicted on me...revenge is usually futile because it can never adequately compensate us for the

> hurt we have suffered. Revenge is best left in the hands of God.
>
> However, restitution is our attempt to demonstrate genuine repentance to someone we have wronged. While revenge is the payment we demand from our offender, restitution is the payment we volunteer to another person we have offended.[2]

Neither the four letters from the FDA thanking me for contacting them regarding my reaction to the prescribed medication and the death of Nathaniel nor the long-awaited letter from them in response to my letter to the President claimed any direct motion to investigate or try and improve the pharmaceutical company's warnings and their apparent failing relationship with them. In so doing this, the FDA handed a free reign of terror to the pharmaceutical company attorneys which completely invalidated the FDA's long overdue apology to me.

The following is my "Thank you" letter. I have never sent it, but I print it here.

> *Dear Pharmaceutical Company,*
>
> *You say I had a false memory retrieval. This from your $60,000 paid forensic psychiatrist, whose team gave Nicholas a diagnosis and never met him, and yet Sophie with whom I'd worked with for years was not asked one question by your team of attorneys. Why? What were you afraid of? I stand by what I say. I have no memories of the car accident or what led up to it. You attack me because you say I said I remembered. I said I remembered parts of the horrific panic and frightful hallucinations of that day. The* ***psychosis!*** *You're the educated ones. When in psychosis you are not in reality. You are removed from the presence of reality when you are in that state. So when you claimed I said I remembered, your claim was that I remembered the unreality of that day. So much for your* ***scientific objectivity!***

Funny how you had no special guest appearances read for the abuser's deposition. Too close to home for you?

In addition, your use of George's testimony was abominable. George's doctor's extensive falsification of his medical records and having filled it with inaccurate facts and wrong names was done in order to cover himself and George's already working relationship. Doctor Byrnes was George's doctor during George's custody fight and as George said, he would kill anyone who got in the way of getting his daughter, you found the weak link in George, a would be assassin.

And yet George was used like a pawn in your game of manipulation, because unbeknownst to him, after calling Dr. Byrnes's office and being unable to get a second appointment, I contacted the specialist who originally gave me the diagnosis and asked for a referral which he gave me. Unfortunately, my taking your prescription medication was never interrupted.

Pharmaceutical Company your use of a former FDA official as representing the positive quality of working relations between the industries involved was the ultimate in hypocrisy. Could you please send me a copy of the document he wrote while employed by the Food and Drug Administration. You know the one that James read in the courtroom where he wrote on why the FDA and the pharmaceutical industry should not collaborate because it is a ***conflict of interest!***

Yours truly,

____

PS. I'm finished signing acquisition papers!

When I read the news about the FDA's decision for preliminary warnings only one week after our trial I became angry. I became even more disgusted with the "I don't know" response from the company medical director during the airing of the news show, and at the Federal Government and the pharmaceutical industries' current working relationship. Upon my request for answers as to what led to the deluge of power that was unleashed upon me and my team of attorneys, and how it led to what I felt was the suppression of valuable evidence that was submitted in our case, I discovered PDUFA or as it is affectionately called "pahduhfah."

The acronym PDUFA stands for the Prescription Drug User Fee Act. About 17 years ago the FDA was confronted with the "issue" that they were taking too long to okay and release new drugs for the market. Congress passed pahduhfah, which gave the green light for drug companies to help finance the process of approving new drugs. I wondered if this might not be what took the bite out of the regulating process with the prescription medication? For insight on this issue see the *Reader's Digest* article dated April, 2008, "Strong Medicine"[3] and the July/August 2007 issue of the *AARP Bulletin* article titled, "Is the FDA Doing Its Job?"[4]

Getting Away With Murder?

Immediately after our losing verdict, the FDA released preliminary warnings about the prescription medication. *Perhaps they thought I would once again be vocal about my cause.* One month later the black box ADHD Drug Warning was *rejected*. In the middle of March, a federal advisory panel rejected the proposal that popular drugs were used to treat attention deficit hyperactivity disorder bear the strongest type of warnings for psychiatric risks and cardiovascular risks. This included the prescription medication I was taking when Nathaniel died. How many more people were unnecessarily injured or how many more unnecessary deaths occurred as these necessary warnings teetered in the balance?

> *I don't know. I don't know. I don't know. I don't know.* ***I don't know!***

Valor Still Alive

I am proud to conclude this chapter with an email from one of the youngest attorneys on our team. He also sent it to the team and all of the people on my email list who I had been communicating with throughout the country. It reads as follows:

For those who do not know me, my name is Jason Collins and I was one of the lawyers that Dawn, through Peter and James, was kind enough to select as local counsel for her case. Over the next several days, weeks or even months many of us will question what happened, why the jury did what they did and what, if anything, could have been done differently. I want everyone to know how wonderful a job that Peter and James did in their representation of Dawn and their fight to get justice for Nathaniel.

This was a very tough case in many regards. Peter and James maintained their professionalism and focus despite the attacks on them, Dawn and everyone else who wasn't working for or hired by the pharmaceutical company. They should be extremely proud of themselves regardless of the outcome. I know I'm proud of them.

As a young lawyer, they have given me a glimpse of how true trial lawyers, true civil justice attorneys, should conduct themselves. They have taught me not to back down just because the other side has more money, more power, more resources. Keep fighting for what you believe in because it's the civil justice attorneys who are the working man and woman's last voice, last hope to get justice.

Dawn, you have been an extremely strong and courageous woman throughout the case, especially over the last several weeks of trial. They attacked you, blamed you and accused you; yet you stood tall, maintained your dignity and never broke. I'm proud of you, Peter, James, Catherine, Joseph, your father and Nathaniel are all proud of you. All you ever wanted was your day in Court, your day to tell your story. The company's relentless battle over 5 years to prevent you from your day in Court was unsuccessful. This Jury didn't blame you, attack you or accuse you. Please don't take their verdict personal, as James already told you. Be proud for standing up to them and fighting for what you believed in. I thank you for that.

Trial work is one of the hardest, most stressful and most emotional jobs out there. Trial attorneys are protective of their clients, of the cases and of their cause. We don't always get positive press, positive publicity or positive feedback; but as Peter reminded this Jury in jury selection, it's the trial lawyers that have made our world safer. We won't let one loss defeat our cause or defeat the reason we do what we do.

James and Peter, thanks for the learning lessons, the advice and the tips. Thanks for keeping my fire burning. And, most of all, thanks for being my friend and brother in arms.

With that, I remain
Very truly yours,
Jason Collins

One of Dawn Marie's Civil Justice Attorneys

March 18, 2001—Flickering Lights

On the one-year anniversary of Nathaniel's death, I had arranged for a Mass to be said for him at St. Bernard of Clairvaux Church. I knew, because I had grown up Catholic, that Masses offered for the deceased are to help them get into heaven. I had no doubt this is where my son was, but to honor his life and provide an opportunity for my family to share in our memories I had it arranged and invited several close friends. There were about fifteen of us present.

As the prayers for petition began to be read, the deacon loudly and clearly announced (which doesn't always happen at this time), "**This Mass is being offered for Nathaniel Joseph Branson!**" Then something unusual began to happen. After the deacon's announcement, the lights began to flicker on and off. At first we all just thought it was a technical thing, but as it began to happen more randomly, my parents and I wondered if it wasn't a sign from Nathaniel—just months before his passing, he'd discovered the light switches!

Then it stopped for a while until the priest began the prayers of consecration of the Holy Eucharist. The lights then went out and stayed out until the moment the priest raised the Host saying, "This is my body given up for you." At that very moment the lights came on and remained on, without a flicker, for the rest of the Mass.

After the Mass we gathered in the lobby and everyone commented on the flickering and the beauty of the Mass. Then the guardian of the church walked our way. We stopped and asked her if flickering lights were a regular or recent occurrence. She told us that it never had happened before. Furthermore, she said that she went into the room with the electrical equipment and fuse boxes and everything was working just fine. We all smiled and I thanked Jesus for allowing Nathaniel to give us this special kiss of consolation from heaven.

EIGHT

HIS TRUTH IS MARCHING ON

—JULIA WARD HOWE

ONE DAY AS MY HUSBAND AND I prayed the scriptural rosary, I was struck by the following verse: "And all at once the angel of the Lord, descending from heaven, came and rolled away the stone and sat on it." (Matt 28:2) I had the image of a magnificent luminous angel of immense strength descending from heaven and rolling away with ease the giant stone that covered the entrance to Jesus's tomb. Then what did this majestic creature do? He sat on it! He sat on the stone! Why include this verse? Was he taking a break? Oh no. He was making a loud statement by this action, because it is of a most significant importance. *It doesn't end here!*

When I was in the fifth grade I had the opportunity to take a field trip to the local courthouse in Wilkes-Barre, Pennsylvania. I will never forget the emotion that struck me at that young age when Mrs. Watson walked us into the courtroom. As I looked at the strong features of the baroque carved cherry wood table which the judge would sit behind, and saw the rows of chairs in which the jury would sit and the location of the witness stand, and the almost altar-like rail that separated the attorneys' tables from the judge, I was swept up in unspeakable awe. I scanned every crevice of the room, taking it in, thinking to myself this is what democracy and the freedom of what my country stands for has been built upon—*Justice for all.*

I felt so proud to be an American. I was struck by how the courtroom reminded me of a church—having an altar-like table where the judge sat, a jury section where the choir might sit, pews where the people would sit and a witness stand where a pulpit might be. Perhaps the two are not so far apart: whereas the courtroom secures justice and peace on earth, our churches secure justice and peace for our eternal salvation. Why I wonder, do the two have to be so zealously opposed to each other?

And when you stand praying, if you hold anything against anyone, forgive him, so that your Father in heaven may forgive you your sins.
—Mark 11:25

As the months went by after the trial and the hurtful realization came to me as to the extent to which the pharmaceutical company used George's false testimony to lay the destructive foundation of their case, I became enraged at the system and most especially at George.

I heard it preached all my life, if you don't forgive you won't be forgiven. *You can't really mean this Lord! This guy doesn't have a conscience!* I also heard we should love our enemies. *Lord, that doesn't sound like a suggestion. What you're asking of me is way too much!*

I've read that when we don't forgive, it's the person who doesn't forgive who suffers and not the perpetrator. I heard at conferences that life is too short and too valuable to waste being bound to feelings of unforgiveness.

I knew with all my heart it was true. I couldn't imagine or conceive that it was possible to forgive the person who stood in the way of justice for Nathaniel and for the other children and adults whom I hoped could have been helped. So I did what I'd always done when

I'd see a mountain before me. I fell to my knees and prayed, begging God for help in this seemingly impossible task. *Lord God, you said that your burden is easy and that your yoke is light...well right now I feel pretty crushed by the burden of bitterness, anger and resentment, and yet I know this is not your will for me. Please help me Good God, to forgive George for what he has done.*

It was not long after these prayers that I received a phone call from my good friend Elizabeth. She had recently attended a talk given by Sister Ann Shields in California. Sister's talk was about... yep, you guessed it, forgiveness. Elizabeth dropped off a CD of the talk for me. The timing couldn't have been better. I listened to the CD almost immediately. Sister made some amazing points in her talk. She began with a quote given by John Paul II during the World Day of Peace. Our Holy Father said, "Forgiveness is not the opposite of justice. Forgiveness IS the opposite of resentment and revenge." Then, after a few more critical points on the difference between justice and forgiveness, Sister Ann Shields began to tell the following true story which is found in *Chicken Soup for the Christian Soul.* You may have heard this story before. For me it was my first time. It had a positive impact on me:

> There is a town located here in Northern California that is called Grass Valley. Well in Grass Valley a number of years ago, there was a priest who was working on his homily for Sunday and a great storm had come up and it was kind of a flash flood situation, a lot of water and a lot of rain. The roads were covered in water and right around midnight the lights went out and he was working on his homily. So he's sitting there with a candle trying to complete the work that he needed to do when the phone rang and it was from a nurse from a hospital in Auburn about thirty five miles away. There was a hospital there in Auburn and the nurse said, "Father, there is a man here dying. Would you come to him? He's asking

for the last rites." Father said, "I'll do my best to get there." It took him two-and-a-half hours. He said later how he couldn't figure out how the road went clear and he got through, and how roads got shut down behind him and he was remarking to himself about this but he didn't put it all together. So he got to the hospital. He went in and he said, "I understand that you would like to receive the last rites," and the man began to swear at him and told him to get the hell out...he didn't want to have anything to do with him. So the priest just went back and sat down in the back of the hospital room and didn't say anything and just sat there. And about a half hour later he went up to the man again and the man cursed and swore and told him to get out...and he went back and he sat down again and he waited two hours. And he walked back up and by now it was early morning and the man looked up and he said, "Well I don't have very long now so they can't get me now." And the priest didn't know if he was hallucinating or what was going on and he said to him, "Do you want to receive last rites? Do you want to go to confession?" And he said, "Yes." And he said, "Father, thirty-five years ago I was drunk and it was Christmas Eve, and I was a switch man on a train, and I went out and I switched it the wrong way... and the train just went onto the wrong tracks, and it hit a car that was going across because the car thought that it was clear." He said, "I killed a man and I killed a woman and I killed their two little girls...and I've hid out in the mountains for the last number of years." He said, "I guess but now my time is ended now and I guess they can't get me now." And the priest said to him, "I forgive you." And the man said, "Well what do you have to do with it? You know. Is God going to forgive me?"

> And the priest said, "Yes, God forgives you," and he gave him absolution and prayed over him. Then he said to him, "Let me just tell you one thing. If I can forgive you God will forgive you. That was my mother and my father and my two sisters."[1]

After hearing this story I was humbled. The seeds were planted. If this priest could forgive such a terrible wrong maybe I could do it. Just maybe I could forgive George.

Then I emailed one who had walked the walk. I emailed a woman named Katherine. I was introduced to Katherine through one of the employees at my parents' design business. Katherine's son Bryan was brutally shot and murdered by a young man named Chris Parker. Chris had brought a gun to a high school party and as he walked around acting invincible, according to witnesses, he instigated fights with whoever got in his way. Unfortunately, Bryan was in the wrong place at the wrong time. Katherine made the following heartfelt suggestions to me concerning forgiveness.

> *Dear Dawn,*
>
> *"If we do not forgive, we are the prisoner. It does not mean we must go to them face to face or have a loving relationship or even a relationship at all with them.*
>
> *A friend almost had me convinced that I never really forgave this person because I did not go face to face or even write a letter. Sometimes we cannot do it on our own. It is only through the grace of God it happens anyway. We must ask God to help us to forgive through our Lord. We cannot accomplish it on our own. Most especially if someone has hurt us so very deeply the feeling of unforgiveness can come back but we can rest assured that Our Lord will be there to help us. We must make the step to ask our Lord for His help and strength. It is a choice...and only we must ask for the help.*

Life is difficult, nevertheless we must look for the ending (eternity). Keep trying to reach where God wants you. The world wants us to be distracted and not trust God, but ourselves....

STOP...PRAY...LISTEN...to our Lord and He will guide you. Dawn you will be in my prayers and please pray for me!"

His peace and joy,
Katherine

I believed that to confront George would be dangerous and that I would probably never find resolution with him face to face. Then the thought came to me to pray a nine-day novena. I chose to pray a novena to St. Theresa the Little Flower because I remembered Saint Padre Pio often spoke fondly of her. *What could it hurt?* I thought.

Shortly after listening to the rest of Sister's talk and reading Katherine's email, I began my novena for the specific intention of completely forgiving George for everything he'd said and done. Every day I would pray that God would allow me to forgive him and that God would bless and heal him. It was a very difficult nine days.

On the final day of the novena I received a special grace. I felt immense peace and a complete release of my pain and anger toward George. I could actually pray for him without bitterness in my heart and prayed that God would bless him on his journey. Until this very day I can sincerely say that I hold no bitterness toward him and am grateful to God for this grace.

This was not all that was to happen that day. When early evening arrived I checked my email and noticed I received an urgent message from my girlfriend Connie. As I read it, I could hardly believe my eyes! Connie sent me an email regarding an article that was all over the headlines. I searched on the FDA's Website to verify its accuracy. It stated: "FDA Directs ADHD Drug Manufacturers to Notify Patients about Cardiovascular Adverse Events and Psychiatric Adverse Events." Included in the fifteen medicines that were to revise labeling and provide black box warnings was the prescription medication that had wreaked so much devastation in my life. The day was Ash Wednesday 2007, which was the beginning of Lent, the very season in which Nathaniel died seven years earlier. I truly felt relief that the warnings were finally going to get out there to the medial profession and their patients!

Sharing The Gift Of Sight

When my parents felt I was strong enough they gave me the following letter. Almost immediately after Nathaniel died, Bill and my parents were approached by a caring representative. My son's death resulted in a generous act.

DONOR NETWORK OF ARIZONA

March 28, 2000

Dear Dawn,

My name is Julie Thompson. I am the Family Services Coordinator at Donor Network of Arizona. On behalf of everyone here let me extend to you our deepest sympathies on the tragic loss of your son Nathaniel. There are not adequate words to offer you at this time. I know the death of a child is the most difficult thing to bear. You remain in our thoughts at this time.

Let me also convey our heartfelt thanks to you for the compassion of your donation. It's humbling to us that even in the midst of your profound grief you were able to choose to help others. Hope for many sightless people depends on the thoughtfulness of individuals like you who are able to think beyond their own grief and sorrow to help others. Many people worldwide are afflicted with blindness. Each year, corneal donation impacts thousand of people in the United States and abroad. Thank you for participating in a mission that offers the gift of sight to others. Because of your thoughtfulness, we were able to restore sight to two individuals. I am able to share with you at this time some basic information regarding these recipients. One of the recipients is a 51 year old woman from the Phoenix area.

The other recipient is a 37 year old woman, also from the Phoenix area. On behalf of these individuals, for the gift of sight, I sincerely thank you....

In the weeks and months to come, I do hope you are able to find consolation in the decision you made for donation. In speaking to donor families in the past, I have found they gained some strength and peace from the knowledge that they sought to help others in their time of need. I hope you and your family are able to find that same kind of strength and peace. With true condolences, but in gratitude, I am

Sincerely yours,
Julie Thompson
Coordinator of Family Services[2]

My son's eyes, the very ones I was blessed to see sparkle and to experience the precious joys of life through, continue to give vision now to two very fortunate individuals.

Put on the armor of God so that you may be able
to stand firm against the tactics of the devil.
—Ephesians 6:6

We think that war and terrorism is happening abroad and that it could never happen to us. We are quite naive if we believe in this stance, as we see early on that with the "mysterious" apple in the garden and in the killing of Abel by his brother Cain, what we are capable of when we abuse our free will. As C. S. Lewis wrote in *The Problem of Pain*, "When souls become wicked they will certainly use this possibility to hurt one another; and this, perhaps, accounts for four-fifths of the sufferings of men. It is men, not God, who have produced racks, whips, prisons, slavery, guns, bayonets, and bombs..."[2]

What was my reason for taking to court a multi-billion dollar corporation? I needed for my pain to be heard. My son could no longer speak for himself. I had a strong need to fight for him.

I will never forget the emotion that struck me as I watched the movie *The Count of Monte Cristo* during my legal crisis. I had watched the movie several times before because it was one of my favorites, but at this particular moment in time there was a line in the movie that struck a cord so deeply in me it was as if I had heard it for the first time.

One of the main characters of the story, Edmund Dantes, was betrayed and unjustly imprisoned for life and sent to an island that housed a European-style Alcatraz. On his prison wall could be seen the words etched into stone by the previous prisoner, "God will give me justice." This seemed to give Edmund solace for a time. Every year, on the anniversary of his arrival, he would receive a brutal whipping on his back. After his beating by the warden he would be escorted back to his dreary stone-block cell, not having human contact until the next year. And as such, when that human contact came, it was without mercy.

Every so often, Edmund picked up a stone and etched over the words of justice, assuring they remained to give him hope…a hope which seemed to escape from him with every passing year.

After the seventh year and a failed attempt to kill himself, Edmund curled up in the corner of his cell, crying like a child, when through the center floor of his stone cell burst an old man who thought he had dug a hole to the outer wall. As Edmund and this fellow prisoner, who he called "priest," discussed their situation, his new friend saw the inscription on the wall and repeated, "God will give me justice," to which Edmund quickly replied there would be no talk of God there. The priest asked why? Edmund replied that God had faded from his heart. His fellow prisoner asked what had replaced it, to which Edmund quickly responded, REVENGE. The priest's reply resonated with me in a way that it never had before: "Perhaps your thoughts of revenge is serving God's purpose of keeping you alive these seven years." To which Edmund responded, "To what end?" and the priest said, "ESCAPE."

I had experienced something so terrifyingly dreadful, something I had never before experienced in the side effect of "psychosis," which resulted in the even worse experience of the sudden death of my precious son. These lines made perfect sense to me now and I realized that the Lord in His graciousness allowed me to be placed in the middle of an unimaginable fight, just as what had happened to me was unimaginable. The investment of five-and-a-half years of my life into this painful process was perhaps what kept me, like Edmund's character, alive during those trying and difficult years.

A Few Words I Wish To Share

Chuck, take the blinders off and stop using the justice system to further your career while destroying the lives of others. Your icy, calculated words may have stung and your slander knocked me down a bit, but I choose to live the reality that life is a millisecond next to eternity and it doesn't end here. Susan, your cunning enabled you to use the justice system to your ends. So it did for Madalyn Murray O'Hare, but we unfortunately know how her story ends. I do appreciate the concern you expressed to Peter for me at trial's end. But as Peter said, not to worry, because I'm one tough son of a ______.

Food and Drug Administration and Pharmaceutical Industry, I forgive you...*but I don't trust you*. Constructive change is necessary for both organizations to heal and grow from the downward spiral in which greed has taken it. Do whatever it takes to regain the attribute of scientific objectivity that is a must in creating better quality pharmaceuticals and products for your client base. Oh, and if you are unaware who these clients are, they're called *human beings!*

Congressmen and Senators, United States Supreme Court Justices and Commander in Chief, use common sense and start passing laws that are just and stop selling your souls to the lobbyists. Protect our democracy, the less fortunate and those who cannot speak for themselves.

"Then render to Caesar what belongs to Caesar's
and to God what belongs to God's."
—Matthew 22:21

James and Peter, I meant what I said when I told you I would rather have been represented by you a hundred times over and lost than to have won by the other side because of their unethical bull____. You believed in me and in my little boy and I can never thank you enough for all you did to defend our rights.

To those of you on the front lines of the battlefield, I thank you and I believe with all my heart that God our Father in Heaven thanks you, too. I offer you these thoughts. Thoughts on how Christ fell under the weight of the cross on His way to Mount Calvary. Remember that when He fell He fell forward, in the direction of His destination, our redemption. He taught us that life is a process and not always perfect. Had life been perfect our Savior would have redeemed us from the manger, but He walked the walk to show us that it can be done, that life *doesn't end here*, and that we are not alone!

Four days after the FDA black boxed the prescribed medication and like medications, it approved a new amphetamine based prescription drug to treat ADD and ADHD. It's a brand new name on the market. It's maker—the same pharmaceutical company!

...persevere and remember, to:

Keep on charging...loving the enemy so long as there is Life

Nathaniel's merciful heart.

Nine

Freedom!

—William Wallace

When I am asked by well-meaning persons if I have any desire to push forward and appeal the case, I say to them I have no desire to fight anymore. Not at least in that realm. It is not because I am beaten; Lord only knows the fires He's placed in my heart are far from being quenched. No, my desire is not to fight back but to work for PEACE, and not just any peace. No, I desire to fight for the peace that surpasses all understanding, the kind of peace that sets aside anger and bitterness at injustice and enacts the love of Christ to work toward true and substantial change for the future generations.

Saint Padre Pio, that dear man and priest who knew personally the depths of human suffering, both in his body and from the masses of humanity who sought him out for healing and cures, had a dream. After many obstacles and immeasurable difficulties his dream was finally realized. It was to build a massive monument, a large hospital with the most advanced facilities to care for and heal the sick. Upon the day of the inauguration of The House for the Relief of Suffering, or as the hospital is affectionately called, "The Casa," he spoke the following words to the doctors and practitioners:

You have the mission of curing the sick but if you do not take love to the beds of the sick I believe medicine is of little use. I have experience of this when my doctor gave me a word of comfort above all else. Love can't work without words. How can you express this other than with words that raise the sick spiritually. Take God to the sick, it is worth more than any other cure.[1]

Saint Maria Goretti offered the ultimate act of peace to mankind through her priest on her deathbed, July 5, 1902, as she told him that she forgave Alessandro Serenelli, her murderer. Alessandro was a young man who brutally and mortally wounded Maria by stabbing her fourteen times when Maria was only eleven years old. Because Maria firmly refused to give in to his sexual advances he got more aggressive, and in a fit of rage grabbed a blunt object. Maria screamed to him, "No Alessandro, don't do this you will lose your soul. Please, don't do this, you will lose your soul Alessandro."[2] She was concerned for his salvation and not for herself! In a crazed fit he unleashed his anger upon her. Eventually, he was found guilty and imprisoned although he initially denied all charges, which were instigated by his attorneys to say that she framed him.

Years into his imprisonment Maria appeared to Alessandro in a dream. At this time he was still refusing to show remorse for his crime. In the dream, Maria handed him one white lily at a time from a beautiful garden of white lilies until she handed him a total of fourteen, the number of times that he stabbed her. Something about this dream spoke deeply to Alessandro and the next morning he called for the guards to get him in touch with the local bishop. He poured his heart out to the bishop, attesting to Maria's purity and profound religious practice. Maria's name was then cleared.

Now here's why I mentioned this incredible story in the first place. St. Maria Goretti's actions set into motion another great miracle. Upon Maria's canonization as a saint, her mother forgave Alessandro everything. Alessandro, upon his release from prison, dedicated the final years of his life to humble service to God as the caretaker of the local monastery grounds!

Nobody, no person, no culture, no religion or race is beyond the loving and merciful redemption of Our Lord Jesus, and I dare say no institution. Oh, I will work for peace and justice, one can be sure. I am not going away; for obvious reasons the Lord left me to wait and work. When I had a strong urge to write and tell Nathaniel's story shortly after trial's end I was told by a few well-meaning friends to let it go. I took their advice and let it go for a while, and during that time I fell in love and married, yet amidst much joy the desire to write about Nathaniel and my fight for justice never left me.

Then I received encouragement from my husband and I tried to write but could not. I asked our Blessed Mother and our Father in Heaven what I should do, for I seemed to lack the courage to put pen to paper. Once again I was sent a sign that filled me with the hope and courage that it could be done. Once again my sign came through the humble servant, Saint Padre Pio.

For years I struggled when I saw a picture of Nathaniel that was placed in the fleur de lis covered gate that surrounded the tomb of Padre Pio. After Nathaniel's death, two dear friends of mine asked if they could take Natheniel's picture with them as they traveled to different shrines throughout Europe and eventually to the burial place of Padre Pio in San Giovanni Rotondo, Italy. Behind Nathaniel's picture lay the impenetrable black granite encasement for the saint who'd suffered so many years for our Good God and His people. Dear God, I prayed, I don't understand how it could be that St. Rita was incorruptible, as well as St. Bernadette of Lourdes, who looks like a sleeping child in her crypt, but not our dear Padre Pio who suffered so willingly and so much. The dear Padre himself tried to put a stop to the tomb they were building for him while he was yet alive: "Remember that when I die, I want a simple burial under the soil! I do not want to be buried in this crypt! I am a worm, a sinner, you must place me under the soil! Have you understood? And don't forget!" These were his words to Padre Carmelo Durante, who oversaw the project. Padre Pio was so adamant about this wish that he began to cry.[3]

As I stood frozen before my computer with a blank page before me wondering if I were nuts to even try and take on a subject such as this story, I checked my email and there was one with an attachment from my dear friend Sarah. Reading the email and the attachment beheld for me the inspiration I needed to proceed. This email contained pictures of the recently exhumed body of Saint Padre Pio, with hands and feet completely healed and looking tender as a baby's skin, the very hands and feet which for 50 years bore the scoring wounds of the crucified Christ. Once again I knew that all things were possible with God, and so I began my task, which I wrote with joy and painful abandon into the wee hours of many nights.

By default I have learned a lot about life and death during this journey, and that although it is inevitable, death is not something to be feared. One of my favorite conversations regarding the subject of eternity was recorded in the book *The Visions of the Children* by best-selling author and attorney Janice T. Connell. Jan shares a strange experience she had while in Medjugorje with her family. In a question and answer session she asked the visionary Vicka about it.

Q. *Vicka, today a strange thing happened at the Mass.*

A. *Which Mass?*

Q. *The nine A.M. German Mass. When we (her family included) walked into the church [Saint James], the whole sanctuary was filled with a mist. We could only see the top of the heads of the priests who were concelebrating the Mass. It was quite unusual. In fact, there was a mystical reality about the Mass. It was like seeing a cloud resting on the floor of the sanctuary and all those who were standing in the sanctuary were standing in the cloud. Do you know anything about that?*

A. *You saw that with your eyes?*

Q. *Yes.*

A. *You had the "veil" lifted from your eyes during that Mass. The "cloud" you saw was really the splendor of all the angels who always surround the altar when the Mass is celebrated.*

Q. *Vicka, how do you know that?*

A. *Everyone knows that! The angels are very much a part of our everyday world. They understand better than we do the holiness of the Eucharist. The angels know who is present. We only know by faith.*[4]

So matter-of-factly Vicka responded to Jan. I love it! It was as if she said don't you understand; this happens at every single Mass we attend—the angels, the cohort, the communion of saints, our loved ones and family members—the *other* reality is really reality! They are all there as they are all here with us in our hearts, because the Kingdom of Heaven resides inside each one of us, especially through the reception of Holy Eucharist. We are not alone, we never were. We need to stop listening to the lies of fathead, the devil, for we are blessed and we must march forward and know and believe without a shadow of a doubt that *It Doesn't End Here.*

A Final Letter Dated March 18, 2008

Dear Family and Friends,

I am not sure anybody is listening any more but I have need to share my voice. I thank those of you who throughout the years have responded in your own special ways to acknowledge the pain of my loss. It helped me to know I was still alive. Numbness can be frightful and deafening. To acknowledge and feel pain is life. Your acknowledgement both blessed me and honored the life of my son.

Today marks the eight year anniversary of my son Nathaniel Joseph's death. To be quite honest I am shocked that I made it this far. I can remember after Nathaniel died arriving home from the hospital, frightened by the emptiness of the home, thinking there was no possible way I would live past another day...and here I am. Now that's a miracle! I think of all the people and places I have met and visited along this journey and I am astounded by the goodness of God. Like Simon there were many who helped me carry my cross and may God bless you for it!

I won't go into a long sermon as I have done in the past because there is not much more to say. I am finding the peace the Lord so longed to give me. I have a wonderful husband and a much anticipated future. As well I have an incredible, loving and supportive family who stuck with me through it all. Importantly I have incredible memories of a little boy who lived for only a short time but gave me a lifetime worth of laughter and wisdom.

Nathaniel lives because Christ lives!

I love you my family and friends and pray you experience in this amazing season of our faith an outpouring of Grace beyond all measure. Let us open our hearts because it is only ***through*** *the big and little deaths of our lives we are brought to the Resurrection.*

Happy Easter!

Dawn Marie Roeder

I received the largest response ever to any of my previous emails. I guess people are still listening.

AFTERWORD

HERE IT IS, THE END, or should I say the beginning; as I look back at the journey and what I have written. Being at a different place when I first began the journey to write, I had always held concern that I may wound another with my words, because I take the written and spoken word very seriously. Why?

Because what we say has great impact. Why do we speak of the Son of Man as the Word come down from Heaven and the Holy Scriptures as the Word of God and that the Word became Flesh. The answer to that question is quite beyond my understanding but it does speak to me something of great importance and that is that God would choose to call Himself the Word. Words can heal or hurt.

I have decided to stick with love.
Hate is too great a burden to bear.
—MARTIN LUTHER KING JR.

In her book *A Simple Path* Mother Teresa says, "There is only one God and He is God to all; therefore it is important that everyone is seen as equal before God. I've always said we should help a Hindu become a better Hindu, a Muslim become a better Muslim, a Catholic become a better Catholic."

Blessed with the opportunity to serve the elder poor and refugees in Bosnia-Hercegovina many years ago, I joined with St. Joseph the Worker organization in the former Yugoslavia with its founder Sister Muriel. We fed not only Catholic families but also Muslim and whoever else needed food or basic medical supplies. Poverty has no elite. The thankfulness of one family and their embrace of Sister Muriel and the volunteers was as genuine and sincere as the other. One little Muslim grandma made certain my hands held a few of her homemade cookies on my way out the door as she beamed with gratitude from our visit. This moment continues to bring a smile within my heart. We prayed with each family to the one God.

I wrote *It Doesn't End Here* from my own experience as a Catholic who loves her faith. A Catholic who was trying desperately to understand the tragedy in which she found herself. I am grateful to all who make up this story, yes even Charles, Susan, my Godfather and George as they are a part of my journey and have helped me realize much about my faith and myself. Although I don't agree with their actions, nor how the system dealt the blows, I hope through this story to raise awareness that change is necessary, and that in order for change to arrive we must turn with all of our hearts and minds, all of our strength and souls, to the One and only God who can bring that change about. (Colossians 3:1, 10–13)

I end with the Mother of God's own words, to us, her children.

Our Lady's September 2nd, 2009 Message To Mirijana Soldo

"Dear children! Today, with a motherly heart, I call you to learn to forgive, completely and unconditionally. You suffer injustice, betrayals and persecutions, but by that you are closer to and dearer to God. My children, pray for the gift of love. Only love forgives all, as my Son forgives—follow Him. I am among you and am praying that when you come before your Father you can say: 'Here I am Father, I followed your Son, I had love and forgave with the heart, because I believed in your judgment and trust in you.' Thank you."

ACKNOWLEDGMENTS

FIRST I WOULD LIKE TO THANK God, the Father, Son and Holy Spirit, for your mercy and enduring love and compassion. When things seemed the worst you cried with me, encouraged me and strengthened me. Thank you for the precious gift of hope that was always available for the asking in which you carried, inspired and called me onward.

To the Blessed Virgin Mary, my beloved Mother, without your example, guidance and tender love I could not have walked this journey. Thank you for the lessons learned and for always being at my side.

To my beloved hero, my husband, Robert, who supported my desire and passion to write this book when he knew the energy, emotion and time it would require of me. Thank you Robert for your love and for always challenging me to live to the fullest "Failure is Not an Option."

I am forever grateful to my family, my mom and dad for having stood unwaveringly by my side through my grief and my fight. You lost your only grandson but never lost the heart to lose your only daughter. Thanks for duking it out for me and with me.

I would like to thank Alison, Carla and Julie for walking closely with me those very early years after my son's death. You truly are the sisters I wish I had always had. You kept Nathaniel alive for me in your willingness to let me share my joys and sorrows so soon after his passing and throughout the years. Your openness to share his presence in your own lives and the lives of your families through his "quiet visitations" keeps a smile on my face knowing he is lovingly looking after you and yours.

With a grateful heart I thank the many people who encouraged me, counseled me, loved me and held me up when I was sometimes unable to do so for myself. For discretionary reasons I do not formally name you here but many of you will have recognized yourselves in the previous pages. I am eternally grateful.

Thank you to Father John Fitzgerald who took the time to read what was supposed to be a gift to him and turned out to be a gift to me. Your "read through" and advice is gratefully valued and your encouragement that I move forward meant the world to me.

To my attorneys and team, what can I say, we gave it one heck of a fight didn't we. I have no doubt Nathaniel is smiling down big from heaven for all you did to honor his life and for his mother.

To Patricia L. Brooks, founder of Scottsdale Society of Women Writers. If it weren't for your wonderful organization and for your taking the time out to meet with me personally, I may never have had the courage to put pen to paper in the first place.

To Pamela Goodfellow, when I came to you with my manuscript I struggled, wondering how this book could possibly help anybody else. I was fortunate to have your constant faith in my ability to tell my story with dignity and love. Your unswerving compassion and scholarly counsel meant the world to me. For this I cannot thank you enough.

Andrea Markowitz thank you for your expertise in the last stages of editing. I am grateful for your enthusiasm over my project and your endearing faith that it will find its readership.

Steve and Linda Voita, I truly appreciate the gift you expressed in the artwork you created, a black-and-white version is included on page 12, across from the Seven Sorrows. Thank you for taking the time to meet with me and listening with your heart to the message I hoped to convey. The painting is beyond my expectations.

Finally last but by no means least thank you Nathaniel for being the twinkle of my eye and for your precocious spirit that continues to bless and inspire me. Please give a big hug for me to our Heavenly Father for the gift he has given me through your life and love.

Endnotes

Chapter Two

1. Faye Harden, "Sudden Accidental Death" *A Journey Together* *http://www.bpusastl.org/images/Sudden_Accident_Death.pdf.* (accessed July 30, 2009).

Chapter Three

1. Dan B. Allender, Ph.D., *The Wounded Heart: Hope For Adult Victims Of Childhood Sexual Abuse* (Colorado Springs, CO: NavPress, 1990), 112.
2. Saint Maria Faustina Kowalska, *The Diary: Divine Mercy in My Soul* (Stockbridge, MA: Marian Press, 2003), 560.
3. *http://www.padrepiodevotions.org/chronology.asp.* (accessed July 16, 2009).
4. Pope John Paul II, *Evangelium Vitae/The Gospel of Life* (Vatican City State/Washington, DC: United States Catholic Conference, 1995), 177.
5. Barbara D. Rosof, *The Worst Loss: How Families Heal from the Death of a Child* (New York, NY: Henry Holt and Co., Inc., 1994), 193.

Chapter Four

1. Padre Pio of Pietrelcina, "What Sustained the Woman," *Magnificat* 6:5 (2004): 73. Reprint from *Letters, Volume II, Correspondence with Raffaelina Cerase, Noblewoman*, 1914–1915.

Fr. Gerardo Di Flumeri, O.F.M. Cap., Ed. (Our Lady of Grace Monestery, San Giovanni Rotondo, Italy, 1997).

Permission to use the above quotes is granted by:
National Centre for Padre Pio, Inc.
Harry E. Calandra, President
2213 Old Route 100, Barto, PA 19504

Chapter 5

1. *http://www.Medjugorje.org/* (accessed June 25, 2009).
2. Mirjana Stanislava Vasilj-Zuccarini, *Our Lady's Call from Medjugorje,* 10th edition

   email: mirjana@ime_screens.com
   phone: 00387-36-651-151
   email: vita@tel.net.ba
   online bookstore: wwwmedjugorje.org/books.htm
   ISBN: 8808424-099-9
3. Songs and Lyrics
   Lee Greenwood, *Proud to be An American.*
4. Jiong Li, M.D., Ph.D., Thomas Munk Laursen, M.Sc., Dorthe Hansen Precht, M.D., Ph.D., Jørn Olsen, M.D., Ph.D., and Preben Bo Mortensen, M.D., "Hospitalization for Mental Illness among Parents after the Death of a Child," *The New England Journal of Medicine* 352:12 (2005): 1190–1196, *http://content.nejm.org* (accessed July 15, 2009).
5. "What is EMDR?" EMDR International Association, Austin, Texas. Shapiro, F. (1989). Efficacy of the eye movement desensitization procedure in the treatment of traumatic memories. *Journal of Traumatic Stress Studies,* 2, 199–223. For more information, see *www.emedria.org.*
6. *L'Osservatore Romano,* 20:1894 (2005): 11, *http://www.vatican.va/news_services/or/or_eng/* (accessed July 30, 2009).
7. Henri J. M. Nouwen, *The Inner Voice of Love* (New York, NY: Doubleday, 1998), 3.

8. Padre Pio of Pietrelcina, *Letters, Volume II, Correspondence with Raffaelina Cerase, Noblewoman*, 1914-1915. Fr. Gerardo Di Flumeri, O.F.M. Cap., Ed. (San Giovanni Rotondo, Italy: Our Lady of Grace Monastery, 1997).

   Permission to use the above quotes is granted by:
   National Centre for Padre Pio, Inc.
   Harry E. Calandra, President
   2213 Old Route 100 Barto, PA 19504

Chapter Seven

1. Dan B. Allender Ph.D., *Bold Love* (Colorado Springs, CO: NavPress, 1992), 186, 187.
2. Robert Jeffress, *When Forgiveness Doesn't Make Sense* (Colorado Springs, CO: WaterBrook Press, 2000), 118, 119.
3. Alexis Jetter, "Strong Medicine: An RD special report on what's ailing the FDA and what it means for you," *Reader's Digest* April (2008), 119–131.
4. Patricia Barry, "Is the FDA Doing Its Job?" *AARP Bulletin* Volume 48 Number 7 July/August 2007 *www.aarp.org/bulletin*.

Chapter Eight

1. Sister Anne Shields, *There Are No Coincidences* in Jack Canfield, Mark Victor Hansen, Patty Aubery, Nancy Mitchell, Chicken Soup for the Christian Soul, (Deerfield Beach, Florida: Health Communications, Inc., 1997), 6.
2. Donor Network of Arizona, 201 West Coolidge, Phoenix, Arizona 85013 602-222-2200 1-800-94-Donor.
3. C.S. Lewis, *The Problem of Pain*, (New York, NY: Macmillan Publishing Co., Inc., 1962), 89.

Chapter Nine

1. Jansen Media and Nova-T, *Padre Pio Sanctus* (2003). *www.janson.com/dvdcatalog/2009/04/28/padre-pio-sanctus/* (accessed September 30, 2009).

2. The Mercy Foundation, *Fourteen Flowers of Pardon: The Life and Death of Saint Maria Goretti*, 1995. *www.ignatius.com.*

3. Padre Carmelo Durante, "Crypt or No Crypt? A personal memory of Padre Pio's reactions to the plan," *The Voice of Padre Pio*, 30:11 (San Giovanni Rotondo, Italy: Our Lady of Grace Capuchin Friary, 2000), 12.

4. Janice T. Connell, *The Visions of the Children* (New York, New York: St. Martin's Press, 1992), 116.

Sorrow Endnotes

First Sorrow

1. Luke 2:32
2. Luke 2:34
3. Isaiah 53:9
4. Luke 2:35
5. Luke 2:51

Second Sorrow

1. Luke 1:30-32
2. Matthew 1:20
3. Luke 1:42-43
4. Luke 2:51

Third Sorrow

1. Isaiah 53:5
2. Psalms 130:1-2a
3. Luke 2:47
4. Luke 2:51

Fourth Sorrow

1. Isaiah 53:7
2. Luke 2:51

Fifth Sorrow

1. Luke 23: 18-25
2. Luke 23:33
3. Genesis 22:2
4. Roy H. Schoeman. *Salvation is from the Jews,* (Roy Schoeman: San Francisco, California: Ignatius Press, 2003), 19.
5. Isaiah 53:5
6. John 19:34
7. Luke 2:51

Sixth Sorrow

1. Luke 2:51

Seventh Sorrow

1. Elisabeth Kübler-Ross Foundation. Ken Ross: *http://www.ekrfoundation.org/* (accessed July 31, 2009).
2. Luke 1: 26-38

I CREATED THE FOLLOWING LIST to help my family and me take an active part in the healing process. These steps were inspired by Al-Anon and A.A.'s 12 steps.

12 Step Aid In The Healing Journey Of Trauma And Severe Loss

1. We admitted we were powerless over strong feelings of grief and sadness and that our lives sometimes felt unbearable to manage.

2. Despite our anger and feelings of not being in control of our loved ones death, we made a choice to believe a Power greater than ourselves could restore our hope and sanity.

3. Made a decision to accept the reality that our child/loved one went home and was not coming back in the way we knew them before.

4. Made a fearless and searching inventory of the blessings our loved ones left behind: memories, gifts & learnings.

5. Admitted to God, to ourselves and to another fellow survivor that we made mistakes just as those who have not suffered sudden loss or trauma.

6. Were entirely ready to allow God to forgive us for not being the perfect person, parent, spouse or loved one.

7. Humbly asked God to help us accept ourselves for who we were at the time of our loss because we know our child/loved one would want us to.

8. Made a list of all the people we felt let us down or contributed to the death of our child/loved one.

9. Made a decision to forgive these persons, organization or circumstances, including ourselves and release the bitterness, pain and resentment to the loving God for healing.

10. Made a conscious effort to care for our whole person, which includes our physical, emotional, intellectual and spiritual needs.

11. Give permission to ourselves to laugh and enjoy life without shame or guilt.

12. Celebrate the life of our child/loved one in a meaningful, tangible way and courageously carry this message of hope and joy to others.

While these adapted Steps are inspired by the Twelve Steps of Alcoholics Anonymous, they are not an adaptation. Rather, they were created specifically by the author, published here, and should not be construed otherwise. A.A., which is a program concerned only with recovery from alcoholism, is not in any way affiliated with this publication.

Resources

THE FOLLOWING IS INFORMATION AND RESOURCES I found helpful along my journey. Inclusion of these resources does not imply endorsement of views expressed therein. Only each individual can decide what is appropriate and effective for each situation.

Books on Faith and Inspiration

Antall, Richard C. *The Way of Compassion: into the heart of the Seven Sorrows of Mary.* Indiana: Our Sunday Visitor, Inc., 1997.

Devotion To The Sorrowful Mother. Chicago: Tan Books and Publishers, Inc., 2002.

Kushner, Harold S. *When Bad Things Happen To Good People.* New York: Avon Books, 1981.

Groeschel, Benedict J. *Arise from Darkness.* California: Ignatius Press, 1995.

Carter, Edward. *The Pain And The Joy.* Ohio: Faith Publishing Company, 1992.

Nouwen, Henri J. M. *The Inner Voice of Love: A Journey Through Anguish to Freedom.* New York: Image Doubleday, 1998.

Nouwen, Henri J. M. *The Path of Waiting.* New York: The Crossroad Publishing Company, 1995.

Schubert, Linda. *Miracle Hour: A Method of Prayer That Will Change Your Life.* California: Miracles of the Heart Ministries, 2003.

Pasquale, Gianluigi. *Secrets Of A Soul: Padre Pio's Letters To His Spiritual Directors*. Massachusetts: Pauline Books & Media, 2003.

Ruffin, Bernard C. *Padre Pio: The True Story*. Indiana: Our Sunday Visitor Inc., 1991.

Teresa, Mother. *A Simple Path*. New York: Ballantine Books, 1995.

Lewis, C. S. *The Problem of Pain*. New York: Macmillan Publishing Company, 1962.

Paul II, John. *The Loving Heart*. New York: Atria Books, 1993.

Kosicki, George. *Spiritual Warfare: Attack Against the Woman*. Ohio: Faith Publishing Company, 1990.

Schlink, Basilea. *Mary The Mother Of Jesus*. Great Britain: Lakeland, 1996.

Scriptural Rosary. Illinois: Christianica Center, 1989.

MAGNIFICAT magazine. New York: *www.magnificat.com*, 2009/2010.

Books on Forgiveness and Inner Healing

Allender Ph.D., Dan B. *The Wounded Heart: Hope For Adult Victims Of Childhood Sexual Abuse*. Colorado: NavPress, 1990.

Allender, Ph.D., Dan B. *Bold Love*. Colorado: NavPress, 1992.

Cochrane, Linda. *Forgiven and Set Free: A Post-Abortion Bible Study for Women*. Michigan: Baker Book House, 2002.

Culbreth, Sallie. *The Uncaged Project: Soul Strategies to Rise above a Wounded Childhood*. New York: iUniverse, Inc., 2006.

Hampsch, John H. *Healing Your Family Tree: A God-designed Solution For Difficult Problems*. California: Queenship Publishing, 1989.

Jeffress, Robert. *When Forgiveness Doesn't Make Sense*. Colorado: WaterBrook Press, 2000.

Tapscott, Betty and Father Robert DeGrandis. *Forgiveness and Inner Healing.* Texas: Praising God Catholic Association of Texas, 2000.

Thatcher, Bryan and Fr. Frank Pavone. *Rachel Weep No More: How Divine Mercy Heals the Effects of Abortion.* Massachusetts: Marian Press, 2003.

Books on the Loss of a Child

McCracken, Anne, and Mary Semel. *A Broken Heart Still Beats: After Your Child Dies.* Minnesota: Hazelden, 1998.

Rosof, Barbara D. *The Worst Loss: How Families Heal from the Death Of A Child.* New York: Henry Holt and Company, Inc., 1994.

Sanders, Catherine M. *How to Survive the Loss of a Child: Filling the Emptiness and Rebuilding Your Life.* California: Prima Publishing, 1998.

McClafferty, Carla Killough. *Forgiving God: A woman's struggle to understand when God answers no.* Tennessee: Discovery House Publishers, 1995.

Floyd, Gregory. *A Grief Un-Veiled: One Father's Journey through the Death of a Child.* Massachusetts: Paraclete Press. 1999.

Wiersbe, David W. *Gone But Not Lost: Grieving the Death of a Child.* Michigan: Baker Book House, 1992.

Lafakis, Irene Vodantis. *Gladsome Rose: a bereaved mother's journey into faith.* Minneapolis: Light & Life Publishing, 1995.

Dean, Katie Hodge. *Grief's Journey...When a Child Dies (Journal).* California: Dancing Peanut Productions, 2004.

A portion of the proceeds of the sale of this book is going to Maggie's Place.

Maggie's Place is a community that provides houses of hospitality for expectant mothers who are alone or are living on the streets.

More information about this wonderful organization can be found at *maggiesplace.org.*

39822444R00123

Made in the USA
Charleston, SC
17 March 2015